,3

Library of Congress Cataloging in Publication Data

Harmon, Robert Bartlett, 1932-
  Understanding Ernest Hemingway.

  Includes indexes.
  1. Hemingway, Ernest, 1899-1961--Bibliography.
I. Title.
Z8396.3.H47 [PS3515.E37] 016.813'5'2 77-14893
ISBN 0-8108-1074-3

      Copyright © **1977** by Robert B. Harmon

Manufactured in the United States of America

7810122

UNDERSTANDING ERNEST HEMINGWAY

A Study and Research Guide

by

ROBERT B. HARMON

The Scarecrow Press, Inc.

Metuchen, N.J., & London

1977

Dedicated to my sister Gwen

"... Seek ye out of the best books
words of wisdom; seek learning,
even by study and also by faith."
Doctrine and Covenants 88:118

CONTENTS

PREFACE

The reader might well wonder why, with all that has already been written about him, we need another book on Ernest Hemingway. This is especially true with works of a bibliographic nature, given the excellent comprehensive bibliography by Andre Hanneman and those compiled by others.

My reason for creating this particular guide is simple and admittedly selfish. As a librarian I have acquired an interest in reading the works of and knowing more about the lives of the more important creative writers throughout history. Not being specifically trained in the field of literature presented a major stumbling block when I began my search for materials on a specific writer. The library in which I work has much information on just about any author one can name; however, the sources are legion and I found no single adequate guide. The more I searched the more convinced I became that there must be possible a type of guide that would assist people such as myself, in finding various types of information about specific authors within the covers of a single, inexpensive book. My attempt to design such a guide is what follows. I chose Ernest Hemingway to start with because he seemed to exemplify the type of author who had influenced the widest spectrum of readers and writers.

The scope of this work is decidedly selective. The aim has been to cite those materials that will assist the user in choosing what will best suit his needs whether it be biographical, critical or otherwise. I wish to thank Professor Carlos H. Baker of Princeton

University and Professor Jackson J. Benson of San Diego State University for their help. Also much thanks and appreciation go to my colleagues of San Jose State University for their encouragement and advice. And last, but most deeply, to my wife, Merlynn, for her devotion, love, and patience, which sustained by efforts throughout the writing of this book, my love and gratitude.

I hope the user will find this guide a good starting place to gain a deeper appreciation of Ernest Hemingway's contribution to American literature.

R B H
February 1977

I

INTRODUCTION

There are few who will disagree as to Ernest Hemingway's position among the most important writers of the twentieth century. What seems open to debate, however, is the nature and extent of his importance. One measure we can apply is the tremendous influence he has had on modern fiction style. He was a master of the art of narration. There is hardly an important American or European writer after Hemingway that has escaped his influence totally.

Hemingway's influence was not limited merely to stylistic concerns. In a broader sense he became the spokesman for the whole generation which came to consciousness in Western civilization following the First World War.[1] Hemingway was hard-minded and preoccupied with the metaphysical significance of violence and death, along with other qualities that appealed especially to the generation of his younger years. Mostly he tried to write the way people talk. Even today many Americans talk and write in the way Hemingway wrote.[2]

In most of his writing Hemingway was able to convey a sense of place. He accomplished this by close but selective attention to details that would distinguish that place from any other, that would make the reader see the place clearly with the eye of his imagination, that would in effect transport him to that particular ground.[3]

Although it has often been said that Hemingway's style is short, staccato, abbreviated, even simplistic, unadjectival, favoring the normal, the fact is that he was in reality the master of many styles, and did not keep to the one he used successfully in some of the early short stories, or in his newspaper dispatches. Changes in the early style are increasingly visible after about 1930, and a good study could be made of precisely how the transitions were accomplished.[4]

Hemingway's appeal to the general reading public today is perhaps not as great as it was just a decade ago, but his influence is still such that a good portion of that public finds relevance in his writing, especially the short stories. His basic appeal seems to stem from his ability to see and to express what he saw with a great and often unerring precision and force. What he wrote was a reflection not only of what he saw but what he felt while seeing it, or so soon after seeing it that the impression of it stayed fresh in his mind.

The appeal of Hemingway will endure partly because of his style--his alchemy, as he terms it. One must ponder, however, the possibility that what Hemingway has written still remains, in a sense, to be read for the first time. Quite possibly Hemingway achieved something far more difficult than writers in earlier centuries had tried. In an age of spiritual decay and defeat, though he presented honestly the condition of that age, Hemingway yet upheld the goodness, nobility, and spiritual worth of mankind.[5]

NOTES

[1]Donald Heiney, Barron's Simplified Approach to Ernest Hemingway (Woodbury, N.Y.: Barron's Educational Series, 1967), p. 1.

[2]Letter from Professor Carlos H. Baker, Princeton University, March 8, 1976.

[3]Ibid.

[4]Ibid.

[5]Samuel Shaw, <u>Ernest Hemingway</u> (New York: Frederick Ungar Pub. Co., 1973), p. 124.

II

BIOGRAPHICAL SOURCES

BIOGRAPHICAL SKETCH

Ernest Miller Hemingway was born on July 21, 1899, in Oak Park, Illinois, which was at this time a prosperous suburb of Chicago. His father, Dr. Clarence E. Hemingway, was a well-known local physician, and his mother, the former Grace Hall, was a devout Protestant and active church worker.

Hemingway started his writing career early. He edited the high school newspaper and, after graduation, obtained a job as reporter on the Kansas City Star. Before the United States entered the 1914-18 war he went to France as a volunteer in an American ambulance unit. He later enlisted in the Italian Arditi and was badly wounded in an accident near the Austrian border which won him the Croce di Guerra with two citations.

Following the Armistice, Hemingway returned to the United States and married Hadley Richardson, a childhood acquaintance. He tried newspaper work again, this time in Toronto, but a restless postwar disillusionment came upon him, and so he left for Europe. While there he became part of what is known as "the lost generation." That name was created by Gertrude Stein, who along with Ezra Pound and Sherwood Anderson provided the greatest literary influence on Hemingway's early writing.

The Hemingways were divorced in 1927; that same year he married Vogue writer Pauline Pfeiffer. In 1928 Hemingway bought a house and moved to Key

West, Florida, where Patrick was born in 1929 and Gregory in 1932. The shocking suicide of his father in 1928 had a profound effect upon his writing later on.

During the 1930's while a foreign correspondent in Paris Hemingway became involved in the Spanish situation including the civil war, which he covered for the North American Newspaper Alliance.

In 1940, Hemingway and Pauline were divorced, and he married another writer, Martha Gelhorn. They toured China and later took up residence in Cuba near Havana. After the start of World War II, Hemingway volunteered his services and those of his fishing boat, the Pilar, and served with the U.S. Navy as a submarine spotter in the Caribbean. In 1944 as a war correspondent he went barn-storming through Europe with the Allied invasion troops.

Following his divorce from Martha in 1944 Hemingway married Mary Welsh, a Time magazine correspondent. They resided in Venice for awhile after the war but finally returned to Finca Vigia (Lookout Farm) near Havana, Cuba. In 1953 his work The Old Man and the Sea won for him the Pulitzer Prize; the Nobel Prize for Literature followed in 1954.

In January of 1954 Hemingway traveled to Africa and was reported dead after two airplane crashes in two days. He survived, despite severe internal and spinal injuries and a concussion, and read the numerous newspaper obituary notices, noting with great pleasure that they were favorable.

Hemingway purchased a home in Idaho near Ketchum in 1959. But he was not happy, and during 1961 he was periodically plagued by high blood pressure and mental depression. He received shock treatments during two long confinements at the Mayo Clinic in Rochester, Minnesota, but they seemed to be of little help. He died on July 2, 1961, at his home, the victim of self-inflicted gunshot wounds.

SOURCES FOR BIOGRAPHICAL INFORMATION

The above is but a brief biographical sketch. Because of Hemingway's immense popularity and his great impact upon American literature, there is a never-ending wealth of biographical source material from which one can glean factual information and insights about his life.

General Sources: There are numerous biographical sources for American authors. Only a few of the more important of these are cited below.

A1. Benét, William Rose. The Reader's Encyclopedia, 2d ed. New York: Crowell, 1965. 1118p.

A comprehensive work containing brief articles on writers, scientists, philosophers, etc., of all nations and all periods; allusions and literary expressions and terms; literary schools and movements; plots and characters; descriptions of musical compositions and works of art, etc. The second edition emphasizes world literature with special attention focused on areas of growing interest such as Russia. See pages 454-455 for a brief article on Hemingway.

A2. Biography Index; A Cumulative Index to Biographical Material in Books and Magazines. New York: H. W. Wilson, 1947- . vol. 1- .

A quarterly index to biographical material with annual and three-year cumulations. It includes current books in the English language wherever published. All types of biographical material are covered. The index is arranged in two sections: (1) biographees listed alphabetically by last name, giving for each, insofar as possible, full name, dates, nationality, and occupation or profession with index references; (2) index by profession and occupation. There are many citations on Hemingway's life and background.

A3. Browning, David Clayton. Everyman's Dictionary

of Literary Biography, English and American, rev.
ed. London: Dent; New York: Dutton, 1960.
769p.

Gives brief biographical sketches of more than
2,000 authors, including contemporaries. Principal
works with dates are noted, but no critical references.
The short biography of Hemingway is on page 318.

A4.　Kunitz, Stanley Jasspon. Twentieth Century Authors; A Biographical Dictionary.... With Howard
Haycraft. New York: H. W. Wilson, 1942.
1577p.

_____.　_____. First Supplement. New
York: H. W. Wilson, 1955. 1123p.

Popularly written sketches, usually of some
length. Includes bibliographies by and about the author.
The sketch on Hemingway is found on pages 635-636 of
the first volume and on pages 434-435 of the supplement.

A5.　Magill, Frank N. Cyclopedia of World Authors,
rev. ed. Englewood Cliffs, N.J.: Salem Press,
Inc., 1924. 3 vols.

Provides biographical information on many authors. Gives place and date of birth and death (when
appropriate), lists of works, a biographical sketch vary-
ing in length from 200 to 1000 words, followed by a
section of bibliographical references to biographical information. The data on Hemingway are located in volume two on pages 827-829.

Specialized Sources: Included below are works
that are largely biographical which either wholly or in
part deal with Hemingway's life.

A6.　Algren, Nelson. Notes from a Sea Diary: Hemingway All the Way. New York: Putnam, 1965.
254p.

The author describes a trip aboard the freighter Malaysia Mail. There he had the opportunity to ponder and review his personal encounter with Hemingway in Cuba, the values inherent in Hemingway's stories, and other matters.

A7. Anderson, Elizabeth. Miss Elizabeth; A Memoir. With Gerald R. Kelly. Boston: Little, Brown, 1969. 315p.

The third wife of Sherwood Anderson describes her life, mainly in artists' colonies in New York, Paris, New Orleans, and Mexico. Among other writers she discusses her acquaintance with Ernest Hemingway.

A8. Arnold, Lloyd R. High on the Wild with Hemingway. Illustrated with photos. Caldwell, Idaho: Caxton Printers, 1968. 343p.

This reminiscence spans the twenty-three years of Hemingway's visits to Idaho, from 1939 to 1961. The author, who accompanied Hemingway on many outdoor trips, gives all the details concerning guns, ammunition and the hunting expeditions.

A9. Aronowitz, Alfred G. Ernest Hemingway; The Life and Death of a Man. With Peter Hamill. New York: Lancer Books, 1961. 222p.

An overview of Hemingway's life and loves.

A10. Baker, Carlos Heard. Ernest Hemingway; A Life Story. New York: Scribner's, 1969. 697p.

One of the most detailed biographies of Hemingway that has yet been written. Most of the information is drawn directly or indirectly from manuscript sources, including many pages of Hemingway's unpublished work, approximately 2500 of his letters, and at least an equal number of letters to him from friends, members of his family, and chance associates. These materials have been supplemented with numerous interviews.

A11.   Broer, Lawrence R. Hemingway's Spanish Trag-
       edy. University: University of Alabama Press,
       1973. 131p.

       The author attempts to show why Hemingway
was attracted to Spanish attitudes, to identify the direct
influences of Spain on Hemingway's diction, and to ex-
plain the effects of these influences on Hemingway's char-
acterizations and his view of life.

A12.   Callaghan, Morley. That Summer in Paris; Mem-
       ories of Tangled Friendships with Hemingway, Fitz-
       gerald, and Some Others. New York: Coward-
       McCann, 1963. 255p.

       Callaghan recalls his association with Heming-
way and others which provides some insights into Hemingway's Paris experience.

A13.   Castillo Puche, José Luis. Hemingway in Spain;
       A Personal Reminiscence of Hemingway's Years
       in Spain by His Friend. Translated from the
       Spanish by Helen R. Lane. Garden City, N.Y.:
       Doubleday, 1974. 388p.

       This biography of Hemingway, written by a
close friend, a Spanish novelist, is intended as a nos-
talgic tribute to a tormented genius. It ranges from
reminiscences about Hemingway to the author's im-
mediate reactions to Hemingway's death to descriptions of what fascinated Hemingway about his adopted
country.

A14.   Ernest Hemingway, As Recalled by His High School
       Contemporaries. Edited by Ina Mae Schleden and
       Marion Rowls Herzog. Design and production by
       Harry Knaphurst. Oak Park, Ill.: Historical
       Society of Oak Park and River Forest, 1973.
       47p. (Historical Society of Oak Park and River
       Forest. Monograph no. 1.)

       Includes illustrations. Based on a panel
discussion presented to the society on October 29,
1971.

A15.   Escarpit, Obert. Hemingway. Brussels: Ren-
       aissance du Livre, 1964.   154p.

       A general overview of Hemingway's life and
writings in the French language.

A16.   Farrington, Selwyn Kip. Fishing with Hemingway
       and Glassell. New York: D. McKay Co. , 1971.
       118p.

       This book includes an account of Hemingway's
attempt to land a large black marlin for use in the film-
ing of his novel The Old Man and the Sea. It is mostly,
however, a discussion of the commercial long-line fishing industry, and the havoc it has wrought in sport fishing waters.

A17.   Fenton, Charles A.   The Apprenticeship of Ernest
       Hemingway: The Early Years. New York: Octa-
       gon Books, 1975, c1954.   302p.

       This work is a definition of the process by
which Ernest Hemingway transposed a conventional talent into an artistic skill.   It deals mainly with his journalistic background.

A18.   Gurko, Leo.   Ernest Hemingway and the Pursuit
       of Heroism. New York: Crowell, 1968.   247p.

       The biographical portion includes the salient
moments of Hemingway's life focusing on his background,
his friends, his marriages, and the important influences
on his personal and literary life.   It concludes with his
tragic final years and death.

A19.   Hemingway, Gregory H.   Papa: A Personal Mem-
       oir. With a preface by Norman Mailer.   Boston:
       Houghton Mifflin, 1967.   192p.

       Written by Hemingway's youngest son, this book
is a frank view of his famous father.   Hemingway is pic-
tured taking on all comers in an improvised boxing ring
on Bimini or being the first fisherman to land tuna un-
touched by sharks.   He is shown in Sun Valley, Idaho,

hunting with Gary Cooper and acting foolish in the presence of Ingrid Bergman--or in Havana in the 1940's, coaching his eleven-year-old Gregory to tie for the pigeon-shooting championship of Cuba, or rescuing him from a shark, or taking him along on a quixotic subchasing expedition that turned into a matchless summer's idyll. Here are Hemingway's wives and here is his platonic romance with a young Italian noble woman. And here, too, is the darker side of a living giant; the rages, the estrangement from his son, the courting of empty "beautiful people," the merciless erosion of his talent, and the descent into the madness that was his greatest terror.

A20.   Hemingway, Leicester.   My Brother Ernest Hemingway.   Cleveland: World Pub. Co., 1962. 283p.

An intimate biography in which the author uses his own notes, family anecdotes, and the memory of friends to recall his brother. Since Ernest Hemingway did not approve publication of his letters, they are not quoted here but are used as source material and frequently paraphrased.

A21.   Hemingway, Mary Welsh.   How It Was.   New York: Knopf, 1976.   576p.

Includes 24 pages of photographs. An intimate and interesting portrait of Ernest Hemingway written by his fourth wife. This account is filled with exhilarating and harrowing tales, with happiness, with struggle, anguish and courage.

A22.   Herrmann, Lazar.   Hemingway: A Pictorial Biography.   By Leo Lania, pseud.   New York: Viking Press, 1961.   141p.

In this work the text and photos depict Hemingway's life, work, social and intellectual milieu. It is essentially a superficial review of Hemingway's life and writing for ephemeral, casual interest. There is apparently no attempt to correlate the illustrations and the text on the same page so that the two give parallel but separate accounts.

A23.   Hotchner, A. E.   Papa Hemingway; A Personal Memoir.   New York: Random House, 1966. 304p.

   The author was a reporter on a magazine assignment when he first met Hemingway. This account of their friendship describes the last thirteen years of Hemingway's life.

A24.   Hovey, Richard Bennett.   Hemingway: The Inward Terrain.   Seattle: University of Washington Press, 1968.   248p.

   The author discusses Hemingway's inner terrain from the internal evidence provided by consecutive analyses of his themes and pervading motifs and from external biographical testimony.   He considers the significance of recurring juxtapositions of love, death, sex, and violence for his inner conflicts and ultimately his art.

A25.   Isabelle, Julanne.   Hemingway's Religious Experience.   New York: Vantage Press, 1964.   114p.

   The author relates Hemingway's encounters with religion to some aspects of his writings.

A26.   Joost, Nicholas.   Ernest Hemingway and the Little Magazines: The Paris Years.   Barre, Mass. : Barre Publishers, 1968.   186p.

   Complements Fenton's study and discusses Hemingway through his formative years in France when he contributed to the Transatlantic Review and Little Review.

A27.   Kiley, John Gerald.   Hemingway: An Old Friend Remembers.   New York: Hawthorn Books, 1965. 198p.

The author of this posthumously published book first met Hemingway in Paris where he, as editor of the Boulevardier, accepted some of Hemingway's writings. These reminiscences provide no radical new interpretation of Hemingway's life style, but his robust reporting of anecdotes and opinions about and by Hemingway will help some understand the real man a little better.

A28. Klimo, Vernon. Hemingway and Jake; An Extraordinary Friendship. With William C. Oursler. Garden City, N. Y. : Doubleday, 1972. 245p.

"Jake" Klimo's relationship with Hemingway was casual. He was a young sailing buddy of Ernest's younger brother. Leicester Hemingway often met Ernest in Cuba and even worked as a crew member aboard the Pilar in the early 1940's. Klimo's life of riding freight, smuggling, sailing and drifting is recorded by him in this book.

A29. Lewis, Robert William. Hemingway on Love. New York: Haskell House Publisher, 1973, c1965. 252p.

Eros (sex), agape (brotherly love), and romantic love are the evolving parts of Hemingway's love ethic. The author gives the impression that this ethic developed from a destruction of romantic love and through eros to agape, the latter extending to a love of the world itself.

A30. McCaffery, John K. M. , ed. Ernest Hemingway; The Man and His Work. Cleveland: World Pub. Co. , 1950. 351p.

An anthology of collected criticism, containing three personality and eighteen critical studies.

A31. Machlin, Milton. The Private Hell of Hemingway. New York: Paperback Library, 1962. 222p.

A somewhat questionable biography since the

author, a former editor of Argosy, treats Hemingway
as a friend, although he had attacked him in a bitter
article in 1960.

A32.   McLendon, James. Papa: Hemingway in Key
       West.   Miami, Fla. :   E. A. Seeman Pub. , 1972.
       222p.

       This work attempts to trace the gradual trans-
formation of Hemingway from well-known but still quite
regular author to the mythical Papa.   The author indicates that the reader will be able to see Hemingway as
a young man walking the streets of Key West, through
achievement of national fame, and eventually to the mythical status of "Papa. "

A33.   Miller, Madelaine Hemingway.   Ernest Heming-
       way's Sister, "Sunny, " Remembers.   Preface by
       Robert Traver.   New York: Crown Publishers,
       1975.   146p.

       This is a collection of family recollections and
memoirs by Hemingway's next younger sister.   Perhaps
the very ordinariness of the narrator is the book's most
important contribution to our understanding of Hemingway's attitudes toward life and his family.   More than a
hundred personal photographs are also included.

A34.   Montgomery, Constance Cappel.   Hemingway in
       Michigan.   New York: Fleet Pub. Corp. , 1966.
       224p.

       The author follows Hemingway's footsteps as
boy and man, through the upper Michigan he loved early,
and often wrote of later, and examines its possible influences on his fiction, especially some famous short
stories.   Includes three of Hemingway's short stories
originally published in the Oak Park (Ill.) High School
Tabula and here reprinted for the first time.

A35.   Nolan, William F.   Hemingway, Last Days of
       the Lion: Including "Now Never There" (a Poem)
       and Hemingway, A Biographical Checklist.   San-

ta Barbara, Calif. : Capra Press, 1974. 38p. (Yes! Capra Chapbook series; no. 24.)

The author traces Hemingway's last year of life and the events that led up to his tragic death.

A36. O'Connor, Richard. Ernest Hemingway. New York: McGraw-Hill, 1971. 143p.

This account relates Hemingway's experiences to his fiction and brings out the high points of his life, recounting his skirmishes with war, his four marriages, his adventurous travels and his intense love of writing. This book is written mainly for juvenile readers.

A37. Pearsall, Robert Brainard. The Life and Writings of Ernest Hemingway. Amsterdam: Rodopi, 1973. 282p. (Melville studies in American culture, v. 2.)

Mr. Pearsall discusses Hemingway's background and the general nature of his writing style.

A38. Richards, Norman. Ernest Hemingway. Chicago: Children's Press, 1968. 94p.

A general discussion of Hemingway, his life, writings and style written for juvenile readers.

A39. Rink, Paul. Ernest Hemingway; Remaking Modern Fiction. Illustrated by Robert Boehmer. Chicago: Encyclopaedia Britannica Press, 1962. 191p.

A biography of Hemingway written for young readers.

A40. Ritzen, Quentin, pseud. Ernest Hemingway. Paris: Editions Universitaires, 1962. 118p.

Covers the life and times of Hemingway and discusses his writings and their impact on literature. In French.

A41. Ross, Lillian. Portrait of Hemingway. New
York: Simon and Schuster, 1961. 65p.

This portrait originated as a Profile in the New
Yorker in 1950. The author has added a preface telling
of the violent reaction to the article when it was first
published. It immediately conveys to the reader the kind
of man Hemingway was--hard-hitting, warm, and exuber-
antly alive.

A42. Sanford, Marcelline (Hemingway). At the Hemingways; A Family Portrait. Boston: Little,
Brown, 1962. 244p.

This autobiographical book by Hemingway's
eldest sister portrays the Hemingways at Oak Park, Illinois, and Walloon Lake, Michigan, during the thirty-
year period between 1898 and 1928 when the six Hemingway children were growing up. Ernest is presented as
only one member of a numerous, lively, handsome and
closely-knit clan.

A43. Sarason, Bertram D. , comp. Hemingway and the
Sunset. Washington: NCR Microcard Editions,
1972. 279p.

A collection of reminiscences from persons who
knew Hemingway well during his writing days.

A44. Seward, William Ward. My Friend, Ernest Hemingway; An Affectionate Reminiscence. South
Brunswick, N.J.: A. S. Barnes, 1969. 69p.

This reminiscence is a worshipful treatment of
a friendly relationship.

A45. Shaw, Samuel. Ernest Hemingway. New York:
Frederick Ungar, 1972, c1973. 136p.

The author discusses Hemingway's life and development as a writer. He also elaborates on Hemingway's artistry and significance.

A46.   Singer, Kurt D. Ernest Hemingway, Man of Cour-
       age; A Biographical Sketch of a Nobel Prizewin-
       ner in Literature. With Jane Sherrod. Minnea-
       polis: T. S. Denison, 1963. 200p.

         A biographical sketch of Hemingway's life writ-
ten for juveniles.

A47.   _____ . Hemingway: Life and Death of a
       Giant. Illustrated by Ben Kudo. Los Angeles:
       Holloway House Pub. Co. , 1961. 223p.

         A rather sensationalized biography published
shortly after Hemingway's death.

A48.   Sokoloff, Alice Hunt. Hadley, the First Mrs.
       Hemingway. New York: Dodd, Mead, 1973.
       111p.

         The author writes of Hadley's years with Hem-
ingway based on a series of interviews with Hadley and
on a file of letters from Hadley to Hemingway.

III

MAJOR WORKS

Of all the sources about Ernest Hemingway none is perhaps more important than his actual writings. These have been arranged into nine categories. Within each section the titles are listed alphabetically. Where possible variant editions are given along with any relevant guides or books written about a particular Hemingway work.

NOVELS

As a novelist Hemingway had his successes and failures. He produced eight novels, mostly filled with colorful action that was, in many ways, exemplified by his own life style. Throughout the majority of his novels Hemingway's writing is vigorous; he uses short sentences with the accents falling on the essential elements, in easy rhythms with recurrent phrases. The overall effect is of letting the story tell itself under press of emotion.

Some critics say that Hemingway's novels lend themselves to fragmentation so well that the reader wonders whether they might have been better as a series of short stories. No matter what one's opinion might be, the novels do provide a profile of Hemingway's time.

B1.   Across the River and into the Trees (1950).

This is the story of an American army officer's last visit to Italy, where he had fought in two wars. Even though he realized that he had not much longer to

live he had a love affair with a beautiful young countess.
Then, on a last hunting expedition, his death came as he
had expected.

Editions: New York: Scribner's, 1950. 308p.
London: J. Cape, 1950. 254p. New York: Dell Pub. Co.,
1950. 320p. Baltimore: Penguin Books, 1966. 236p.

B2.   A Farewell to Arms (1929).

Lieutenant Henry, an American, is enlisted
with the Italian army on the Italian-Austrian frontier.
He is severely wounded, and while convalescing contin-
ues a love affair he had previously begun with an English nurse, Catherine Barkley.   The story ends in Swit-
zerland where Catherine has a baby, born dead, and she
herself dies a few hours afterwards.

Editions: New York: Scribner's, 1929. 355p.
London: J. Cape, 1929. 349p. New York: P. F. Col-
lier, 1929. 355p. New York: Grosset & Dunlap, 1929.
355p. New York: Modern Library, 1932. 355p. New
York: Bantam Books, 1955. 249p. Baltimore: Penguin
Books, 1958. 255p. New York: Scribner's, 1967. 358p.

Related Materials:

B3.   Biles, J. I. The Aristotelian Structure of
A Farewell to Arms.   Atlanta: Georgia State
College, 1965. 23p.
Discusses the influence of Aristotle's writ-
ing on the structure of this Hemingway novel.

B4.   A Farewell to Arms; A Critical Commentary.   Project editor, Armand Schwerner.
New York: A Study Master Publication, 1963.
42p.
Includes a bibliography on pages 41-42.

B5.   Gellens, Jay, comp. Twentieth Century
Interpretations of A Farewell to Arms; A
Collection of Critical Essays.   Englewood

Cliffs, N. J.: Prentice-Hall, 1970. 121p.
As the subtitle implies, this collection of
essays analyzes the structure and content of
this novel.

B6. Hillegass, Clifton K. A Farewell to Arms;
Notes, rev. ed. Revised by James L. Rob-
erts. Lincoln, Neb.: Cliff's Notes, 1966.
61p.
Intended as a guide for students and includes a bibliography on pages 60-61.

B7. Klibbe, Lawrence Hadfield. Ernest Hemingway's A Farewell to Arms; A Critical Commentary. New York: Monarch Press, 1964.
58p.
Intended as a student guide and includes a
bibliography on pages 55-58.

B8. For Whom the Bell Tolls (1940).

The framework of this novel is a minor inci-
dent in the horror that was the war in Spain. Robert
Jordan is a young American in the Loyalist ranks who
has been detailed to blow up a bridge. His mission
carries him into hill country where he must seek the
aid of guerrilla bands. Jordan destroys the bridge, but
while he is escaping with his companions his horse is
knocked from under him by an exploding shell and he
lies on the hillside, his leg crushed by the animal's fall.
He sends his companions on and waits, with a sub-ma-
chine gun beside him, for the enemy's approach. This
novel contains all the strength and brutality of all the
previous Hemingway books. The scenes are remarkably
vivid and characters are life-like and remain in one's
memory. Because of its frankness in treating certain
incidents, it is not for adolescents.

Editions: New York: Scribner's, 1940. 471p.
New York: Sun Dial Press, 1940. 410p. New York:
P. F. Collier, 1940. 471p. Philadelphia: Blakiston
Co., 1940. 410p. London: J. Cape, 1941. 462p.

Princeton, N. J. : Princeton University Press, 1942.
498p. New York: Overseas Editions, 1944. 470p.
New York: Bantam Books, 1951. 502p.

Related Materials:

B9. Bonneville, Georges. Hemingway, "Pour
qui sonne le glas"; Analyse critique. Paris:
Hatier, 1970. 64p.
A critique and analysis of this novel. Includes a bibliography on pages 62-63.

B10. Cooperman, Stanley. Hemingway's For
Whom the Bell Tolls; A Critical Commentary. New York: Barrister Pub. Co. , 1966.
64p.
Intended as a study guide for students and
includes a bibliography on pages 62-64.

B11. Grebstein, Sheldon Norman, comp. The
Merrill Studies in For Whom the Bell Tolls.
Columbus, Ohio: Merrill, 1971. 122p.
A collection of essays analyzing various
aspects of this novel. Includes bibliograph-
ical references.

B12. Klibbe, Lawrence Hadfield. Ernest Hem-
ingway's For Whom the Bell Tolls; A Critical
Commentary. New York: Monarch Press,
1965. 48p.
Intended as a study guide for students.
Includes a bibliography on pages 47-48.

B13. Islands in the Stream (1970).

This posthumous novel is divided into three
parts: Bimini, Cuba and At sea. Bimini is Thomas
Hudson in the 1930's entertaining the three sons of his
two wrecked marriages. Cuba is Thomas Hudson clan-
destinely aiding the war effort around 1942. At Sea is
Thomas Hudson commanding the pursuit of some German
U-boat survivors.

Editions: New York: Scribner's 1970. 466p.
London: Collins, 1970. 398p.

B14. The Old Man and the Sea (1952).

A brief novel about supreme courage. In the
story an old Gulf fisherman, overtaken by hard luck,
proves his tenacity and courage when he hooks a mon-
ster marlin. He kills his catch but is towed out to sea,
and then he brings what the sharks leave of it back to
Havana.

Editions: New York: Scribner's, 1952. 140p.
London: J. Cape, 1952. 127p. London: Reprint So-
ciety, 1953. 117p. Moscow: Foreign Languages Pub.
House, 1963. 109p. Toronto: Saunders, 1964. 159p.

Related Materials:

B15. Cooperman, Stanley. Hemingway's The
Old Man and the Sea; A Critical Commentary.
With Murray H. Cohen. New York: Barris-
ter Pub. Co. , 1966. 72p.
Intended as a study guide for students and
includes a bibliography on pages 69-72.

B16. Jobes, Katharine T. , comp. Twentieth
Century Interpretations of the Old Man and the
Sea; A Collection of Critical Essays. Englewood Cliffs, N. J. : Prentice-Hall, 1968. 120p.
Contains a collection of interpretative essays on this novel and includes a bibliography
on pages 119-120.

B17. The Sun Also Rises (1926).

In this novel the reader is introduced to a
group of English and American drifters on the contin-
ent who have the means and the time to blow where
they list, from the boulevards of Paris to the bull-
fights of Spain, bathing, eating and drinking much of

the time. In effect this novel relates the hard, acid truth about this group of ineffectuals and conveys the tragedy of their lives, particularly through the futile love of Jake who tells the story, and Brett, the over-sexed Lady Ashley.

Editions: New York: Scribner's, 1926. 259p. New York: Modern Library, 1926. 259p. New York: P. F. Collier, 1926. 259p. New York: Grosset & Dunlap, 1926. 259p.

Related Materials:

B18. Carey, Gary. The Sun Also Rises; Notes. Lincoln, Neb.: Cliff's Notes, 1968. 77p.
Intended as a study guide for students and includes a selected bibliography on page 77.

B19. Cooperman, Stanley. The Major Works of Ernest Hemingway: A Critical Commentary. New York: Monarch Press, 1965. 68p.
See pages 32-41 for a commentary of The Sun Also Rises.

B20. Hillegass, Clifton K. The Sun Also Rises; Notes, rev. ed. Lincoln, Neb.: Cliff's Notes, 1964. 59p.
Intended as a study guide for students.

B21. Klibbe, Lawrence Hadfield. Ernest Hemingway's The Sun Also Rises; A Critical Commentary. New York: Monarch Press, 1965. 76p.
Intended as a study guide for students and includes a bibliography on pages 74-76.

B22. Mizener, Arthur. Twelve Great American Novels. New York: New American Library, 1967. 204p.
The Sun Also Rises is one of the novels discussed in this collection of essays.

B23. To Have and to Have Not (1937).

The scene of this novel is Key West and Cuba. The story is a sort of saga, disconnected and episodic, of one Harry Morgan, burly, surly, hard-nature "Conch" (as Key West natives refer to themselves), whose life has been spent in the single-minded effort to keep himself and his family at least on the upper fringes of the "have nots." As the owner of a fast motorboat, he charters it to big-game fishermen, and also uses it for running contrabnad. On the whole this Hemingway novel is a series of episodes like bombs, told sometimes by the hero, sometimes by others, each one leaving havoc in the reader's mind.

Editions: New York: Scribner's, 1937. 262p. London: J. Cape, 1937. 256p. New York: Grosset & Dunlap, 1937. 262p. New York: P. F. Collier, 1937. 262p. New York: Permabooks, 1956. 180p.

B24.   The Torrents of Spring (1926).

This, the first of Hemingway's novels, is an amusing parody of the school of literature of which Sherwood Anderson is the main exemplar. It tells the story of two workers in the pump factory at Petosky, Michigan, where Hemingway lived briefly when he came back from Italy after the war. The main character is Scripps O'Neil whose drinking habits and two marriages makes a story in itself. In addition to Scripps is his buddy Yogi Johnson who enjoys communing with Indians and has evidently been somewhat traumatized by his experiences in the war. Occasionally Hemingway seems to be satirizing himself, or at least the nihilism and pessimism of the postwar generation whose spokesman he was shortly to become with The Sun Also Rises.

Editions: New York: Scribner's, 1926. 143p. Paris: Black Sun Press, 1932. 176p. London: J. Cape, 1933. 173p. Baltimore: Penguin Books, 1966. 108p. New York: Scribner's 1972. 90p.

(III, Major Works, cont.)

NON-FICTION

In addition to the novels and short stories, Hemingway wrote much of a journalistic nature and some actual accounts of his experiences as a sportsman and observer of the social scene.

B25.   By-Line Ernest Hemingway (1967).

The editor presents a collection of some news features and magazine articles that Hemingway contributed on such subjects as the aftermath of the First World War, the Spanish Civil War, the Second World War, hunting, fishing and writing.

Editions: New York: Scribner's, 1967. 489p. London: Collins, 1968. 479p. New York: Bantam Books, 1968. 428p.

B26.   Death in the Afternoon (1932).

In this particular work Hemingway displays his expertise and knowledge of bullfighting. The book is packed with descriptions of all phases of the institution of bullfighting, from the raising and training of the bulls to sketches of the bullfighters themselves. Throughout the book, at intervals, a singular old lady holds conversations with the author on the subjects of death, modern literature, and sex. The book contains an extensive glossary, a short estimate of the American matador, Sidney Franklin, and many pages of photographs.

Editions: New York: Scribner's, 1932. 517p.

London: J. Cape, 1932. 558p. New York: Halcyon
House, 1932. 517p. New York: P. F. Collier, 1933.
278p.

B27. Ernest Hemingway, Cub Reporter (1970).

These news stories involve prize fights, a
police raid, ambulance runs, an auto accident, Navy
recruitment, and a dance for soldiers. An appendix
lists other reports Hemingway may have written for the
Kansas City Star. This slim volume includes previously uncollected news stories. They are actually only a
small part of his seven months' work for this newspaper
from October 1917 to April 1918. The pieces illustrate
Hemingway's early desire to go beyond straight reporting in his use of color and feeling. Here, too, are important examples of his first attempts to deal with death
and violence in terse prose and controlled sentiment.
The short works show some problems of syntax but
otherwise an unusual amount of maturity for an 18-year-
old writer.

Edition: Pittsburgh: University of Pittsburgh
Press, 1970. 66p.

B28. Ernest Hemingway's Apprenticeship: Oak Park,
1916-1917 (1971).

Here are all of Hemingway's writings for the
Oak Park High School Trapeze and Tabula in 1916-1917
in one collection. This work provides new biographical information about the youthful interests and activi-
ties of Ernest Hemingway. The volume is illustrated
with previously unpublished photographs of Hemingway
and facsimiles of Trapeze and Tabula pages.

Edition: Washington, D. C. : NCR Microcard
Editions, 1971. 122p. (Edited by Matthew J. Bruccoli.)

B29. Green Hills of Africa (1935).

This is an account of a hunting expedition to Africa. In the book Hemingway attempted to write about an actual event to see whether the shape of a country and the pattern of a month's events, if truly presented, can compete with a work of the imagination. In addition to the adventures of the trip, interest is heightened by the fact that all who took part in the hunt were treated as if they were characters in a novel. The book also contains a great deal of literary criticism.

Editions: New York: Scribner's, 1935. 294p. London: J. Cape, 1936. 284p. Garden City, N. Y. : Doubleday, 1954. 199p. Baltimore: Penguin Books, 1966. 243p.

B30. A Moveable Feast (1964).

This posthumous collection of sketches was begun in Cuba in the autumn of 1957 and completed in the spring of 1960. It is a set of short literary reminiscences of the era. Mostly, this is a book about people, and the choice Hemingway made among the many he knew remains perplexing, despite the prefatory note that it was made "for reasons sufficient to the writer."

Editions: New York: Scribner's, 1964. 211p. London: J. Cape, 1964. 191p. New York: Bantam Books, 1965. 209p. Baltimore: Penguin Books, 1966. 159p.

B31. The Wild Years, Ernest Hemingway (1962).

This book is a collection of selected articles written by Hemingway for the Toronto Star between 1920 and 1923. The Star sent him abroad to cover disturbances in the Near East, and about 1921 he settled in Paris where he met Gertrude Stein, Ezra Pound and Sherwood Anderson. In these articles, written in the inimitable Hemingway style, is Paris at her most glorious, Italy and Germany in their darkest hours, the bloody birth pangs of new nations in the Near East and many other events.

   Edition: New York: Dell Pub. Co. , 1962.
288p. (Edited and introduced by Gene Z. Hanrahan.)

(III, Major Works, cont.)

SHORT STORIES

As a creative writer Ernest Hemingway was a master of the short story. This is evidenced by the many anthologies in which such examples as "The Killers" and "The Undefeated" appear. In his short stories even more than in his novels, there appears the well-known "Hemingway dialogue" that has been characterized as inimitable, though often imitated, short, clipped, and bare, using only essential words to convey his message.

B32.   The Fifth Column and the First Forty-Nine Stories (1938).

This volume contains a full-length play, The Fifth Column, and a complete collection of Hemingway's short stories up to the date of publication. Included in this collection of short stories was The Snows of Kilimanjaro, one of his most popular works.

Editions: New York: Scribner's, 1938. 597p. New York: P. F. Collier, 1938. 597p. London: J. Cape, 1939. 590p.

Related Materials:

B33.   Fowler, Austin. Hemingway's The Snows of Kilimanjaro, New York: Monarch Press, 1966. 78p.
Intended as a study guide for students and

includes a bibliography on pages 75-78.

B34. Hillegass, Clifton. The Snows of Kiliman-
jaro, and Other Stories by Ernest Hemingway;
Notes Including Individual Story Summaries and
Commentaries, Selected Examination Questions.
Lincoln, Neb.: Cliff's Notes, 1964. 56p.
Intended as a study guide for students.

B35. Howell, John M., comp. Hemingway's
African Stories; The Stories, Their Sources,
Their Critics. New York: Scribner's, 1969.
169p.
Includes a research anthology of The
Snows of Kilimanjaro.

B36. In Our Time (1924).

The first issue of this collection consisted of
a series of vignettes or sketches, most of them less
than a page long and most of them concerned with the
First World War or with bullfighting incidents. The
American version includes these vignettes, two stories
from Three stories ... and Ten Poems plus ten new
stories.

Editions: Paris: Three Mountains Press,
1924. 300p. New York: Boni & Liveright, 1925. 214p.
London: J. Cape, 1926. 248p. New York: Scribner's,
1930. 212p.

B37. Men Without Women (1927).

This book contains fourteen short stories, each
one pared down to the absolute minimum of description.
Ten of these short stories were previously published and
four were new ones. All of them are written in Hemingway's admirably clean and incisive style. Every page
manages to picture the reality of life. As to the emo-
tional or artistic value of the pictures, readers' opinions
naturally differ.

Editions: New York: Scribner's, 1927. 232p. London: J. Cape, 1928. 221p. Cleveland: World Pub. Co., 1946. 164p. Baltimore: Penguin Books, 1955. 160p.

B38.   The Nick Adams Stories (1972).

This work is a collection of all the stories in which the character Nick Adams plays a role. The stories are arranged chronologically, not as they were written, but as the events they describe occur.

Edition: New York: Scribner's, 1972. 268p.

B39.   Short Stories (1956).

This volume brings into one collection forty-nine of Ernest Hemingway's short stories. There are tales of the war years, and impressions of modern life. This collection is essentially the same as number B32 except that it excludes his play, The Fifth Column.

Edition: New York: Scribner's, 1956. 799p.

B40.   Three Stories: Up in Michigan, Out of Season, My Old Man & Ten Poems (1923).

Hemingway's stories, sketches, and other short fiction pieces have been published in other volumes under various titles. In general these collections are cumulative, that is, each one includes the stories of the previous volume and adds later materials. This collection was the first of these volumes.

Edition: Paris: Contact Pub. Co., 1923. 58p.

B41. Winner Take Nothing (1933).

Of the fourteen short stories contained in this volume some have appeared in periodical form, but the majority are here published for the first time.

Editions: New York: Scribner's, 1933. 244p. London: J. Cape, 1934. 250p.

POETRY   PLAYS   FILM SCRIPT

Out of the mountain of material written about
Ernest Hemingway, one area which has received relatively little attention from the critics seems to be his
poetry.   What is perhaps most enlightening about Hemingway's poems is not so much their quality, but their
chronology.   Hemingway apparently wrote poems throughout his life, most frequently in Paris days and earlier,
and then again after World War II, but also during the
later twenties and thirties.

B42.   Collected Poems (1960).

Originally published in Paris, this is a pirated
edition.   There is some question as to the comprehen-
sion of this collection.

Editions: San Francisco: 1960. 28p. New
York: Haskell House, 1970. 28p. New York: Gordon
Press, 1972. 28p.

B43.   Three Stories ... and Ten Poems (1923).

This work was the first appearance of Hemingway's poems in a collection.

Edition: Paris and Dijon: Contact Publishing
Co. , 1923. 58p.

Related Material:

B44.   Wagner, Linda Welshimer.   Hemingway

and Faulkner. Metuchen, N. J. : Scarecrow
Press, 1975. 297p.
    The Appendix I (pp. 237-242) includes a
discussion of Hemingway's poetry.

    Along with not being recognized for his abilities
as a poet, Ernest Hemingway was also not renowned
for his dramatic works.

B45. The Fifth Column; A Play in Three Acts (1938).

    This play tells of counter-espionage against
the fascists' secret "column" inside Madrid, which aid-
ed the four military columns aimed at the city. Hemingway weighs one's responsibility "only to yourself" as
against responsibility to society, the attractions of love
and life at international resorts as against dedication to
the Loyalist, Communist cause. Throughout the play,
Hemingway's commitment to the cause of humanity remains slightly hypothetical.

    Editions: New York: Scribner's, 1938 (in-
cludes the first forty-nine stories). New York: Scribner's, 1940. 101p. Harmondsworth (Eng.): Penguin
Books in association with J. Cape, 1966. 95p. London:
J. Cape, 1968. 106p.

B46. Today Is Friday (1926).

    This one-act play was Hemingway's first ex-
periment with drama. Three Roman soldiers are talk-
ing in the wineshop of a Jew about the routine crucifix-
ion they had just performed.

    Editions: Englewood, N. J. : The As stable
Publications, 1926. 7p. New York: Scribner's, 1938.
(This play has appeared in several collections of Hem-
ingway's short stories.)

    Following is the only film script written by

Ernest Hemingway.

B47. The Spanish Earth (1938).

       This film scenario was written for a documentary movie on behalf of the Spanish peasant. Hemingway collaborated with director Joris Ivens and photographer John Ferno in making this film.

       Edition: Cleveland: J. B. Savage Co. , 1938. 60p. (With an introduction by Jasper Wood, illustrations by Frederick K. Russell.)

(III, Major Works, cont.)

AS EDITOR   COLLECTIONS   UNPUBLISHED

Following is the only collection of others' essays
edited by Ernest Hemingway.

B48.   Men at War (1942).

Hemingway edited and wrote the introduction to
this anthology of eighty-two stories and factual accounts
about wars and their effect upon man from Biblical times
to the Second World War.   The arrangement is topical
by divisions suggested in the classic On War by von
Clausewitz.

Editions: New York: Crown Publishers,   1942.
1072p.   New York: Brumhall House, 1955. 1072p.   New
York: Berkeley Pub. Corp. , 1958. 505p.   London:
Collins, 1966. 383p. (shortened version).

The collections listed below include various com-
binations of Hemingway's writings.   This list is not complete; however, those works cited are among the more
well-known, anthology-type publications that have been
complied by various editors.

B49.   The Enduring Hemingway; An Anthology of a Lifetime in Literature.   Edited with an introduction
by Charles Scribner Jr.   New York: Scribner's,
1974. 864p.

A thematic arrangement including selections

from novels, some complete short stories and other journalistic articles.

B50.   Ernest Hemingway, Knut Hamsun [and] Hermann Hesse. New York: A. Gregory, 1971. 378p.

The first part of this collection includes Hemingway's Nobel Prize acceptance speech along with the presentation address. Also includes "A Clean, Well-lighted Place," excerpts from "The Old Man and the Sea," "The Sun Also Rises," "A Farewell to Arms," and an essay entitled "The Life and Works of Ernest Hemingway."

B51.   The Essential Hemingway.... London: J. Cape, 1964, c1947. 447p.

Contains one complete novel, excerpts from three others, twenty-three short stories and a chapter from Death in the Afternoon.

B52.   Hemingway. Edited by Malcolm Cowley. New York: Viking Press, 1944. 642p.

This work is one of the Viking Portable Library series. It includes four novels and six stories.

B53.   The Hemingway Reader. Selected, with a foreword and twelve brief prefaces, by Charles Poore. New York: Scribner's, 1957, c1953. 652p.

Includes the complete text of The Sun Also Rises along with excerpts from other major novels, non-fiction and ten short stories.

Hemingway left behind a relatively large corpus of unpublished material, some of which has already been published. In a recent interview, Ernest Hemingway's widow, Mary Hemingway, indicated that she would not have any of Ernest's writings published that do not equal or surpass the writings published in his lifetime.

The writings that have yet to be published include a full-length novel entitled The Garden of Eden and some half-dozen stories and articles.

IV

SOURCES OF CRITICISM

AND INTERPRETATION

The flow of Hemingway criticism and interpretation has been enormous and shows no sign of abating. The scholarly journals, for example, continue to publish serious essays on Hemingway. The origin of this critical and interpretative literature is not strictly limited to English-speaking countries but is quite international in scope. That Ernest Hemingway was one of the major figures of American literature is indicated by the fact that in terms of quantity there is more writing about his work than the author himself ever produced.

It is perhaps rather obvious that criticism of Hemingway's writing has been both positive and negative. Hemingway, himself, was often irritated, to put it mildly, with those "schoolmarm" critics who insisted on rapping his knuckles for supposed moral reasons instead of looking at his writing as literature. As one writer has indicated whether for praise or blame, Hemingway critics and interpreters seem to have agreed on one thing, that he was one of the great literary figures of our time.

Of the sources for criticism or interpretation of Hemingway's works, books and periodicals are the most productive for the student. The first place to begin one's search is the card catalog of the library for reference and book materials. For periodical articles there are several indexes that will be of great value. These are cited and annotated below.

GENERAL

There are a number of general sources other than the card catalog that include references to Hemingway criticism along with other authors. Three of these are discussed below.

C1. Combs, Richard E. Authors: Critical and Biographical References; A Guide to 4,700 Critical and Biographical Passages in Books. Metuchen, N.J.: Scarecrow Press, 1971. 221p.

Over 4,700 criticism and biographical references to some 1,400 authors are listed in this work, and 500 books containing literary criticism are analyzed. Each reference cited is in English and is at least six pages in length. Part I, Author Citation, lists authors alphabetically. Part II, Key to Symbols, lists alphabetically by symbol all the analyzed books. Symbols and full bibliographical citations are given. Part III, Author Index to Books Analyzed, arranges the 500 books by author, giving title and symbol.

C2. Contemporary Literary Criticism. Edited by Carolyn Riley. Detroit: Gale Research Co., 1973- . Vol. 1- .

Contains criticism and evaluations of both new and established modern authors now living, or deceased since 1960. Each entry includes lengthy excerpts from one to a dozen or more appraisals of an author's work taken from both major and minor reviewing media; excerpts may treat one of the author's works or his entire canon. Each volume in the series covers about 200 authors in 600 to 700 pages and includes a cumulative index. New authors and playwrights as well as important older writers whose work is not widely covered in critical sources are prominently featured.

C3. Curley, Dorothy Nyren, comp. Modern American Literature, 4th enl. ed. Edited and compiled with Maurice Kramer and Elaine F. Kramer.

New York: Frederick Ungar Pub. Co. , 1969.
3 vols.

This source book and index excerpts hundreds
of critical books, essays, articles, and reviews dealing
with the work of nearly 300 important twentieth-century
American novelists, poets, dramatists, and essayists,
with citations to original sources.

BOOKS

A rather large number of individual works of a critical nature are available on Hemingway. Some of the titles below are collections of criticism. The list below is only selective.

C4. Asselineau, Roger, ed. The Literary Reputation of Hemingway in Europe. With an introduction by Heinrich Straumann. New York: New York University Press, 1965. 210p. (includes bibliographies).

These eight papers given at the symposium on Hemingway which constituted one session of the 1960 Working Conference of the European Association of American Studies, trace the history of the critical and popular response to Hemingway's work in England, France, Germany, Norway, Sweden, the U.S.S.R., Italy and Spain. Indicates the striking diversity of views which reveal the literary consistencies of the nations involved.

C5. Atkins, John Alfred. The Art of Ernest Hemingway. New York: Roy Publishers, 1954, c1953. 245p.

A British critic's evaluation of Hemingway's personality and his writing style.

C6. Baker, Carlos Heard, ed. Hemingway and His Critics; An International Anthology. Edited, with an introduction and a checklist of Hemingway

criticism. New York: Hill and Wang, 1961.
298p. (includes bibliography).

In his selection and introduction the editor
emphasized the international aspects of Hemingway's
career and reputation. The checklist of criticism is
very useful.

C7. _____. Hemingway; The Writer as Artist,
4th ed. Princeton, N.J. : Princeton University
Press, 1972. 438p. (includes bibliographical
references).

The more or less "definitive" work on Hemingway. The emphasis, as the subtitle suggests, is on the
writer as artist, rather than the man as writer. Professor Baker's chief concern is the critical examination
and illumination of each of Hemingway's works. Between the chapters devoted to the novels, short stories
and nonfiction appear essays in interpretation of Hemingway's philosophy.

C8. Baker, Sheridan Warner. Ernest Hemingway;
An Introduction and Interpretation. New York:
Holt, Rinehart and Winston, 1967. 150p. (bibli-
ography, p. 137-142).

A judicious biographical and critical treatment. Includes an analysis of Hemingway's works set
against the background of his life.

C9. Benson, Jackson J. Hemingway; The Writer's
Art of Self-Defense. Minneapolis: University
of Minnesota Press, 1969. 202p. (bibliographical footnotes).

In this study of a number of the short stories
and five of the novels, the author discusses Hemingway's use of satire, irony, and humor to achieve his
goals.

C10. Brooks, Cleanth. The Hidden God; Studies in
Hemingway, Faulkner, Yeats, Eliot, and Warren.

New Haven, Conn. : Yale University Press,
1963. 136p.

The author's thesis is that more first-rank
modern literary works than realized--and particularly
the books of his chosen five writers--embody a hidden
Christian component, a starkly imaginative confronta-
tion of reality which, broadly interpreted, testifies to
the importance of a substratum of Christianity.

C11. De Falco, Joseph. The Hero in Hemingway's
Short Stories. Pittsburgh: University of Pittsburgh Press, 1963. 226p.

In this study the author is preoccupied with
Christian symbolism in which his interpretations of individual stories are often overwrought.

C12. Donaldson, Scott. By Force of Will; The Life
and Art of Ernest Hemingway. New York: Viking Press, 1976.

This is a different sort of book about Heming-
way--not a biography, not a personal memoir, but a
study of his character, comparing the attitudes and i-
deas he presents in his novels with the ones he actually lived. Fame, money, sports, politics, war, mas-
tery, love, sex, friendship, religion, art, and death--
Donaldson pays full attention to the contradictions in
each field, but ends by suggesting an underlying pattern in the character of this fear-haunted young man
who became a world-famous author by force of will.

C13. Grebstein, Sheldon Norman. Hemingway's
Craft. With a preface by Harry T. Moore.
Carbondale: Southern Illinois University Press,
1973. 245p. (bibliography, p. 234-259).

The author has arranged his study of Hemingway hewing to a strict line of discussion on style,
structure, narrative, perspective, dialogue, and humor.
This book, concentrating on the texts, lucidly explains
the technical means by which Hemingway achieves his

effects.

C14. Hemingway in Our Time. Edited by Richard
Astro and Jackson J. Benson. With an introduction by Jackson J. Benson. Corvallis: Oregon State University Press, 1974. 214p. (includes
bibliographical references).

This collection of twelve hitherto unpublished
essays presented at the 1973 Hemingway Conference of
Oregon State University concerns works such as the
posthumous novel and stories which have been less ex-
haustively discussed than the major novels.

C15. Howell, John M. , comp. Hemingway's African
Stories; The Stories, Their Sources, Their Critics. New York: Scribner's, 1969. 169p. (includes bibliographical references).

Provides complete texts, their background and
critiques. Includes suggested topics for controlled and
library research.

C16. Kaushal, Jogendra. Ernest Hemingway: A Critical Study. Patiala, India: Chandi Publishers,
1974. 143p. (bibliography, p. 135-137). [Not
examined.]

C17. Killinger, John. Hemingway and the Dead Gods;
A Study in Existentialism. New York: Citadel
Press, 1965. 114p.

First published in 1960 by the University of
Kentucky Press. In this study of Hemingway's fictional
world as related to the world view of existentialism,
the author contends that Hemingway's interpretation of
life is strikingly parallel to the views of such European
writers as Sartre, de Beauvoir, and Camus.

C18. McCaffery, John K. M. , ed. Ernest Hemingway;
The Man and His Work. Cleveland: World Pub.
Co. , 1950. 351p.

An anthology of collected criticism, containing three personality sketches and eighteen critical studies.

C19.   Nahal, Chaman Lal.   The Narrative Pattern in Ernest Hemingway's Fiction.   Rutherford, N. J. : Fairleigh Dickinson University Press, 1971. 245p. (bibliography, p. 235-242).

The author contends that the moment of passivity rather than the moment of action is the real center of Hemingway's work.   He asserts that it is qualitatively different from similar moments in other writers, that it places the Hemingway character in fruitful touch with the dark mystery that surrounds man, and links him with the outer cosmos.   In support of his argument he assembles examples from the novels.

C20.   Peterson, Richard K.   Hemingway, Direct and Oblique.   The Hague: Mouton, 1969.   231p. (bibliography, p. 217-223).

In addition to compiling a cross section of critical views on Hemingway's style and values, the author attempts to show Hemingway's almost pathological distrust of words as being the reason behind the celebrated style, rather than a set of values towards life.

C21.   Reynolds, Michael S.   Hemingway's First War; The Making of A Farewell to Arms.   Princeton, N. J. : Princeton University Press, 1976.   309p. (bibliography, p. 299-304).

Using sources generally unavailable to scholars, the author shows that A Farewell to Arms is based on extensive research, part of a previously unsuspected fictional method.   Drawing on the National Archives of the Red Cross and a personal interview, Reynolds also pieced together the biography of Agnes Von Kurowsky, Hemingway's World War I nurse.   In addition, work with other materials has enabled him to identify many of the sources Hemingway used in writing the novel.

C22. Rovit, Earl H. Ernest Hemingway. New York:
      Twayne Publishers, 1963. 192p. (notes and ref-
      erences, p. 174-183; bibliography, p. 184-188).

          One of the better books discussing the back-
ground of Hemingway along with a critical analysis of
his works.

C23. Sanderson, Stewart F. Ernest Hemingway. New
      York: Grove Press, 1961. 120p. (includes bib-
      liographies).

          A brief and rather broad work interpreting
the dynamics of Hemingway's writing against the background of his life.

C24. Scott, Nathan A. Ernest Hemingway; A Critical
      Essay. Grand Rapids, Mich. : Eerdmans, 1966.
      46p. (bibliography: p. 45-46).

          A critical view of Hemingway's treatment of
religious subjects in his writing.

C25. The Short Stories of Ernest Hemingway: Critical
      Essays. Edited, with an overview and check-
      list, by Jackson J. Benson. Durham, N.C. :
      Duke University Press, 1975. 375p.

          A comprehensive checklist of Hemingway's
short fiction. Criticism, explication, and commentary
are found on pages 311-375. The editor has assembled
from books and periodicals thirty articles of interpretation and criticism written about Hemingway's short
stories. A good collection.

C26. Srivastava, Ramesh. Determinism in Heming-
      way. Amritsar, India: Guru Nanak University,
      1975. 20p. (includes bibliographical references).

          A brief analysis of Hemingway's use of de-
terminism in his writings.

C27. Stephens, Robert O. Hemingway's Nonfiction;
      The Public Voice. Chapel Hill: University of
      North Carolina Press, 1968. 391p. (biblio-
      graphical footnotes).

      A chronological list of Hemingway's non-fiction
is found on pages 347-361. In this book, especially in
its last section, and in an appendix which lists almost
60 further "echoes," the author traces analogues between
Hemingway's articles and his fiction.

C28. Wagner, Linda Welshimer, ed. Ernest Heming-
      way: Five Decades of Criticism. East Lansing:
      Michigan State University Press, 1974. 328p.
      (includes bibliographical references and index).

      These twenty-two essays delineate the develop-
ment of the young writer, Hemingway's own critical
interests, and his continuing emphasis on craft. Although there is a connecting theme, no essay repeats
another, so the variations on that theme are numerous.
The essays are divided into four categories: I, The
Development of the Writer; II, Studies of the Work as
a whole; III, Studies of Method and Language; IV, Studies of Individual Novels. Unlike many collections of
Hemingway criticism, attention is given here to the
many short stories, the two versions of In Our Time,
and For Whom the Bell Tolls, Across the River and
into the Trees, and the later novels.

C29. _____ . Hemingway and Faulkner: inventors /
      masters. Metuchen, N. J. : Scarecrow Press,
      1975. 297p. (includes bibliographical references
      and index).

      Attempts to show the parallels between the
careers of these two major American novelists. Born
near the turn of the century, both men matured during
years of exciting artistic ferment, and their early writing is a direct result of new aesthetic concerns in painting, film, and music as well as in literature. The author devotes her opening chapter to a study of this artistic milieu, and then she traces the development of

each writer chronologically. The later work is shown
to be thematically similar but technically different from
each writer's early fiction, and the author's craft-ori-
ented perspective helps to make these changes in method clear. A relatively new reading of several major
novels results. Her study includes all the major novels and many of the short stories of each man. She
concludes her study with appendices on Hemingway and
Faulkner as poets.

C30. Waldhorn, Arthur, ed. Ernest Hemingway: A
Collection of Criticism. New York: McGraw-
Hill, 1973. 149p. (bibliography, p. 141-149).

A collection of essential criticsm on the
great American novelist.

C31. _____. A Reader's Guide to Ernest Hemingway. New York: Octagon Books, 1975, c1972.
284p. (filmography, p. 265-266; bibliography,
p. 267-278).

This volume is a synthesis of Hemingway's
work and that of his critics. It includes a survey of
Hemingway's genius from the early short stories through
Islands in the Stream. Part I is a presentation of his
life and style. Part 2 details the patterns his writing
took; the maturing hero and the hardening code.

C32. Watkins, Floyd C. The Flesh and the Word:
Eliot, Hemingway, Faulkner. Nashville: Van-
derbilt University Press, 1971. 282p. (includes
bibliographical references).

The author contends that there is a discern-
ible shift in style and technique away from the concrete
objectivity espoused and executed by each of these writers in their youthful works to an abstract moralizing in
the later works. The overall result was a loss of artistic merit.

C33. Watts, Emily Stipes. Ernest Hemingway and the
Arts. Urbana: University of Illinois Press,

1971. 243p. (includes bibliographical references).

This examination of Hemingway's progressive concern with art from his early works through the posthumous work, Islands in the Stream (1970), illuminates the essence of this unique literary technique, a conscious synthesis of painting prose. The author attempts to demonstrate that Hemingway's awakening to art forms in the Paris of the 1920's had a profound effect on his later development as a writer, one who adopted all the colors, textures, and planes of existence expressed by such artists as Cézanne, Goya, Bosch, Brueghel, El Greco, and the Surrealists.

C34. Weeks, Robert Percy, ed. Hemingway: A Collection of Critical Essays. Englewood Cliffs, N. J.: Prentice-Hall, 1962. 180p. (includes bibliographies).

Includes a group of critical essays along with Malcolm Cowley's introduction to the Portable Hemingway (1944).

C35. Wylder, Delbert E. Hemingway's Heroes. Albuquerque: University of New Mexico Press, 1969. 255p. (bibliography, p. 245-252).

This study of the Hemingway hero focuses on the hero as he appears in the individual novels, and considers each novel as a separate entity with its own distinctive artistic unity and its own distinctive protagonist. There is also an analysis of the narrative perspective from which Hemingway told the story. The examination of the separate novels reveals a different emphasis, a picture of Hemingway gradually changing his artistic concepts as the world became more complex.

C36. Young, Philip. Ernest Hemingway. New York: Rinehart, 1952. 244p.

A full-length critical analysis of the whole of Ernest Hemingway's work from the earliest stories through The Old Man and the Sea (1952). This work is an attempt to be a guide to the meaning and value of Hemingway's work.

C37. _____. Ernest Hemingway; A Reconsideration, rev. ed. University Park: Pennsylvania State University Press, 1966. 297p. (bibliographical footnotes).

The author asserts that Hemingway's heroes were modeled on himself and that Hemingway's own life was modeled on the heroes of earlier American classics, particularly Mark Twain.

(IV, Sources of Criticism, cont.)

PERIODICAL LITERATURE

In terms of quantity the periodical literature on Hemingway, particularly that of a critical and interpretative nature, is even more voluminous than book and pamphlet materials. In order to gain access to this vast literature the student should become intimately acquainted with several periodical indexes that are available in most libraries. For articles appearing in more general periodicals, The Reader's Guide to Periodical Literature (1900-) is available. Articles appearing in the more specialized periodicals and scholarly journals can be found in The Humanities Index (April 1974-), formerly the Social Sciences and Humanities Index (June 1965-March 1974), formerly the International Index (1916-May 1965). For articles appearing in British journals the student can consult Subject Index to Periodicals (1915-1961), which has been continued as the British Humanities Index (1962-).

The items on the following list have been selected from the indexes cited above. They represent only a small part of the materials that have been published.

C38.   Backman, Melvin. "Hemingway: The Matador and the Crucified," Modern Fiction Studies, Vol. 1 (August 1955), 2-11.

A very interesting, persuasively argued thematic attempt to locate two major forces in Hemingway's fiction.

C39.   Bishop, John P. "The Missing All," Virginia

Quarterly Review, Vol. 13 (summer 1937), 107-121.

An appreciative essay on the effects of Hemingway's prose.

C40. Carpenter, Frederick I. "Hemingway Achieves the Fifth Dimension," PMLA, Vol. 69 (September 1954), 711-718.

An attempt to demonstrate the relationship between Hemingway's concept of time and the aims of his aesthetic.

C41. Colvert, James B. "Ernest Hemingway's Morality in Action," American Literature, Vol. 27 (November 1955), 372-385.

An analysis of Hemingway's code of morality and a defense of its guiding discipline.

C42. Cowley, Malcolm. "A Portrait of Mister Papa," Life, Vol. 25 (January 10, 1949), 86-101.

A rather journalistic sketch in biography that contains a number of useful facts.

C43. D'agostini, Nemi. "The Later Hemingway," Sewanee Review, Vol. 68 (summer 1960), 482-493.

An analysis of Hemingway's later works.

C44. Friedrich, Otto. "Ernest Hemingway: Joy Through Strength," American Scholar, Vol. 26 (autumn 1957), 410, 518-530.

An intelligent hostile criticism, attacking Hemingway's work on ethical and ontological grounds.

C45. Fuchs, Daniel. "Ernest Hemingway, Literary Critic," American Literature, Vol. 36 (January 1965), 431-451.

Details some of Hemingway's critical writings and discusses his attitude toward criticism.

C46. Fussell, Edwin. "Hemingway and Mark Twain," Accent, Vol. 14 (summer 1954), 199-206.

A comparative study of the uses of "integrity" in the two writers.

C47. Galligan, Edward L. "Hemingway's Staying Power," Massachusetts Review, Vol. 8 (summer 1967), 431-439.

Examines the influence Hemingway has had on critics and readers in general.

C48. Graham, John. "Ernest Hemingway: The Meaning of Style," Modern Fiction Stories, Vol. 6 (winter 1960-61), 298-313.

A good stylistic analysis of Hemingway's work.

C49. Halliday, E. M. "Hemingway's Ambiguity: Symbolism and Irony," American Literature, Vol. 28 (1956), 1-22.

A discussion of Hemingway's "realism," and a useful corrective of misreadings of Hemingway's symbolism.

C50. _____. "Hemingway's Narrative Perspective," Sewanee Review, Vol. 60 (spring 1952), 202-218.

One of the better analyses of Hemingway's narrative perspective.

C51. Hamalian, Leo. "Hemingway as Hunger Artist," The Literary Review, Vol. 16 (fall 1973), 5-13.

Another view of Hemingway as an artist.

C52. Hart, Robert C. "Hemingway on Writing." College English, Vol. 18 (March 1957), 314-320.

A good short summary of Hemingway's aesthetic.

C53. Hoffman, Frederick J. "No Beginning and No End: Hemingway and Death," Essays in Criticism, Vol. 3 (January 1953), 73-84.

A thematic study of Hemingway's attitude toward and use of death in his writings.

C54. Jones, John A. "Hemingway: The Critics and the Public Legend," Western Humanities Review, Vol. 13 (autumn 1959), 387-400.

A good account of the relationship of Hemingway criticism to Hemingway's work in the 1930's.

C55. Kashkeen, Ivan. "Ernest Hemingway: A Tragedy of Craftsmanship," International Review, Vol. V (1934), 76-108.

A Marxist criticism of Hemingway's work.

C56. Levin, Harry. "Observations on the Style of Ernest Hemingway," Kenyon Review, Vol. 13 (autumn 1951), 581-609.

A serious analysis of Hemingway's style, still provocative.

C57. Lewis, Wyndham. "The Dumb Ox: A Study of Ernest Hemingway," The American Review, Vol. 3 (June 1934), 289-312.

A very caustic attack on both Hemingway and his work. It is perhaps the fountainhead of all subsequent similar attacks.

C58. Plimpton, George. "Ernest Hemingway," Paris Review, Vol. 18 (spring 1958), 61-82.

An interview with Hemingway that is somewhat useful for its information and Hemingway's guarded remarks.

C59. Rodger, William. "Immortal Hemingway; Letter and Other Manuscript Material," Hobbies, Vol. 79 (September 1974), 154-155.

A brief look at a Hemingway letter and some other unpublished manuscript material.

C60. Rosenfeld, Isaac. "A Farewell to Hemingway," Kenyon Review, Vol. 13 (1951), 147-155.

An interesting psychoanalytic examination of Hemingway's evasion of feeling and fear of femininity.

C61. Sanders, David. "Ernest Hemingway's Spanish Civil War Experience," American Quarterly, Vol. 12 (summer 1960), 133-143.

C62. Somers, Paul P. "Mark of Sherwood Anderson on Hemingway: A Look at the Texts," South Atlantic Quarterly, Vol. 37 (autumn 1974), 487-503.

Discusses and explores the early influence of Anderson on Hemingway by a comparison of writings.

C63. Wegelin, Christof. "Hemingway and the Decline of International Fiction," Sewanee Review, Vol. 73 (spring 1965), 285-298.

Explores the general decline of international fiction and the effect of Hemingway's writings on this decline.

V

DISSERTATIONS AND THESES

As post-graduate work in our institutions of higher education has been growing at a considerable pace during the past ten years there has been a not unexpected growth in the number of masters' and doctoral dissertations in literature. Some of these are published commercially some time after their submission, and usually in much amended form; most are not. Masters' theses and doctoral dissertations are not primary sources. They represent original research on specific topics and are, for the most part, based on primary materials.

Lists of masters' theses and doctoral dissertations are often quite important for literary research. The student hunting a subject for his thesis or dissertation can find out what topics have already been covered. Similarly, the student hunting information on his subject can find valuable, and often the only, information available, as well as extensive bibliographic information in completed theses and dissertations. Once the student working on his thesis or dissertation and the research worker have located the titles of the theses or dissertations and at what institution they were written, they can arrange to borrow copies through interlibrary loan or to purchase microfilm or xerox copies if they cannot be borrowed.

A good guide to individual lists of masters' theses is Dorothy M. Black's Guide to Lists of Master's Theses (Chicago: American Library Association, 1965). For doctoral dissertations there is a series of works issued by University Microfilms at Ann Arbor, Michigan.

The major part of the series is Dissertation Abstracts International (1969- , issued monthly), which replaced Dissertation Abstracts which appeared between 1952 and 1969 and which was preceded by Microfilm Abstracts, which ran from 1938 to 1951. The abstracts in the current work are quite detailed, but they are limited to those works which are available for sale on microfilm or in a full-size copy, and not all universities permit this. However, as a guide to what can be located with a minimum of difficulty, it is particularly useful--although the broad subject headings make searching in some subject fields time-consuming, or tedious, as the key word index does not necessarily reveal all items on a specific subject. There is currently a multi-volume, cumulative, key-word index that covers up to 1972 for this series of abstracts. A comprehensive list of all dissertations is American Doctoral Dissertations (1957- , issued annually), which is arranged by broad subject headings and subdivided by name of the awarding university. No abstracts are given in this work which is the successor to Doctoral Dissertations Accepted by American Universities (New York: H. W. Wilson, 1934-1956, issued annually). The final work in the University Microfilm series is Masters Abstracts: Abstracts of Selected Masters' Theses on Microfilm (1964- , issued quarterly). This work is quite limited by its selectiveness.

DISSERTATIONS

Doctoral studies on Ernest Hemingway have been particularly numerous. The list below was taken from the works listed above.

D1. Adams, Philip Duane. "Ernest Hemingway and the Painters: Cubist Style in The Sun Also Rises and A Farewell to Arms. " Dissertation Abstracts International, Vol. 32 (May 1972), 6311-14.
    Abstract from a doctoral dissertation, Ohio University, 1971 (217p.).

D2. Alderman, Taylor. "Ernest Hemingway: Four
     Studies in the Competitive Motif. " Dissertation
     Abstracts International, Vol. 31 (July 1970),
     380-A.
     Abstract from a doctoral dissertation, Uni-
     versity of New Mexico, 1970 (156p.).

D3. Baldwin, Kenneth Huntress, Jr. "Autobiography
     as Art: An Essay Illustrated by Studies of the
     Autobiographies of Henry Adams, Ernest Heming-
     way, and Vladimir Nabokov. " Dissertation Ab-
     stracts International, Vol. 31 (January 1970),
     3538-2.
     Abstract from a doctoral dissertation, Johns
     Hopkins University, 1970 (227p.).

D4. Benson, Jackson Jerald. "Ernest Hemingway and
     the Doctrine of True Emotion. " Dissertation Ab-
     stracts, Vol. 27 (May 1967), 3862-A.
     Abstract from a doctoral dissertation, Univer-
     sity of Southern California, 1966 (300p.).

D5. Bobb, Sydney Ralph. "Fighter Against Loss:
     The Hemingway Hero. " Dissertation Abstracts,
     Vol. 14 (June 1954), 974.
     Abstract from a doctoral dissertation, Stanford
     University, 1954 (218p.).

D6. Bovie, Verne H. "The Evolution of a Myth: A
     Study of the Major Symbols in the Works of Ern-
     est Hemingway. " Dissertation Abstracts, Vol. 17
     (May 1957), 1080.
     Abstract from a doctoral dissertation, Univer-
     sity of Pennsylvania, 1957 (304p.).

D7. Brady, Emily Kuempel. "The Literary Faulk-
     ner: His Indebtedness to Conrad, Lawrence,
     Hemingway, and Other Modern Novelists. " Dis-
     sertation Abstracts, Vol. 23 (December 1962),
     2131-2132.
     Abstract from a doctoral dissertation, Brown
     University, 1962 (236p.).

D8.   Broer, Lawrence Richard. "The Effects of
        Ernest Hemingway's Identification with Certain
        Aspects of Spanish Thinking on His Rendering of
        Character. " Dissertation Abstracts, Vol. 29
        (April 1969), 3606-A.
        Abstract from a doctoral dissertation, Bowl-
        ing Green State University, 1968 (156p.).

D9.   Byrd, Lemuel Brian. "Characterization in Ern-
        est Hemingway's Fiction, 1925-1952, with a Dic-
        tionary of the Characters. " Dissertation Abstracts
        International, Vol. 30 (April 1970), 4444-A.
        Abstract from a doctoral dissertation, Univer-
        sity of Colorado, 1969 (519p.).

D10.   Ciholas, Karin Nordenhaug. "Three Modern
        Parables: A Comparative Study of Gide's L'Im-
        moraliste, Mann's Der Tod in Venedig, and Hem-
        ingway's The Old Man and the Sea. " Disserta-
        tion Abstracts International, Vol. 33 (February
        1973), 4404-A.
        Abstract from a doctoral dissertation, Univer-
        sity of North Carolina at Chapel Hill, 1972
        (240p.).

D11.   Crozier, Robert Devereux. "A Study of Heming-
        way's For Whom the Bell Tolls. " American Doc-
        toral Dissertations, (1965), 154.
        Citation refers to a doctoral dissertation pre-
        sented at Loyola University of Chicago, 1965.

D12.   Dahiya, Bihm Singh. "The Hero in Hemingway:
        A Study in Development. " Dissertation Abstracts
        International, Vol. 36 (November 1975), 2818-A.
        Abstract from a doctoral dissertation, Univer-
        sity of Cincinnati, 1975 (346p.).

D13.   Dean, Anthony Bruce. "Hemingway's Fiction:
        A Tragic Vision of Life. " Dissertation Abstracts
        International, Vol. 32 (August 1971), 961-A.
        Abstract from a doctoral dissertation, Temple
        University, 1971 (190p.).

D14. Dean, Sharon Welch. "Lost Ladies: The Isolated Heroine in the Fiction of Hawthorne, James, Fitzgerald, Hemingway, and Faulkner." Dissertation Abstracts International, Vol. 34 (November 1973), 2612-A.
Abstract from a doctoral dissertation, University of New Hampshire, 1973 (254p.).

D15. DeFalco, Joseph Michael. "The Theme of Individualization in the Short Stories of Ernest Hemingway." American Doctoral Dissertations, (1961), 127.
Citation refers to a doctoral dissertation presented at the University of Florida, 1961.

D16. Dubiel, Richard Michael. "Disquietude, Existence, and Endurance: Aspects of Paul Tillich's Thought in Selected Works of Ernest Hemingway." Dissertation Abstracts International, Vol. 35 (December 1974), 3734-A.
Abstract from a doctoral dissertation, Purdue University, 1974 (251p.).

D17. Dunn, Charles William Jr. "Ironic Vision in Hemingway's Short Stories." Dissertation Abstracts International, Vol. 32 (March 1972) 5225-A.
Abstract from a doctoral dissertation, Kent State University, 1971 (225p.).

D18. Elliott, Gary Douglas. "The Hemingway Hero's Quest for Faith." Dissertation Abstracts International, Vol. 34 (November 1973), 2621-A.
Abstract from a doctoral dissertation, Kansas State University, 1973 (162p.).

D19. Farley, Pamella. "Form and Function: The Image of Women in Selected Works of Hemingway and Fitzgerald." Dissertation Abstracts International, Vol. 35 (December 1974), 3635-A.
Abstract from a doctoral dissertation, The Pennsylvania State University, 1973 (245p.).

D20.   Feeney, Joseph John.   "American Anti-war Wri-
       ters of World War I: A Literary Study of Ran-
       dolph Bourne, Harriet Monroe, Carl Sandburg,
       John Dos Passos, E. E. Cummings and Ernest
       Hemingway." Dissertation Abstracts International,
       Vol. 32 (June 1972), 6972-A.

D21.   Gebhardt, Richard Coate.   "Denial and Affirma-
       tion of Values in the Fiction of Ernest Heming-
       way." Dissertation Abstracts International, Vol.
       31 (September 1970), 1274-A to 1275-A.
       Abstract from a doctoral dissertation, Michi-
       gan State University, 1969 (261p.).

D22.   Gladstein, Mimi Reisel.   "The Indestructible
       Woman in the Works of Faulkner, Hemingway,
       and Steinbeck." Dissertation Abstracts Interna-
       tional, Vol. 35 (September 1974), 1655-A.
       Abstract from a doctoral dissertation, Uni-
       versity New Mexico, 1973 (214p.).

D23.   Gleaves, Edwin Sheffield, Jr.   "The Spanish In-
       fluence on Ernest Hemingway's Concepts of
       Death, Nada, and Immortality." Dissertation Ab-
       stracts, Vol. 25 (October 1964), 2511-12.
       Abstract from a doctoral dissertation, Emory
       University, 1964 (180p.).

D24.   Gottlieb, Carole Patricia.   "The Armored Self:
       A Study of Compassion and Control in The Great
       Gatsby and The Sun Also Rises." Dissertation
       Abstracts International, Vol. 32 (July 1971), 429-
       A to 430-A.
       Abstract from a doctoral dissertation, Univer-
       sity of Washington, 1970 (207p.).

D25.   Grant, Naomi M.   "The Role of Women in the
       Fiction of Ernest Hemingway." Dissertation Ab-
       stracts, Vol. 29 (June 1969), 4456-A.
       Abstract from a doctoral dissertation, Univer-
       sity of Denver, 1968 (191p.).

D26.   Greer, John Thomas.   "The Limitations of the

Concepts of Sin and Forgiveness as Reflected in the Writings of Ernest Hemingway." American Doctoral Dissertations, (1968), 253.
Citation refers to a doctoral dissertation presented at the New Orleans Baptist Theological Seminary, 1968.

D27. Grimes, Larry E. "The 'Fifth Dimension': The Religious Design of Hemingway's Early Fiction." Dissertation Abstracts International, Vol. 35 (May 1975), 7306-A.
Abstract from a doctoral dissertation, Emory University, 1974 (389p.).

D28. Grimes, Sister Richard Mary. "Hemingway: The Years with Esquire." Dissertation Abstracts, Vol. 27 (July 1966), 204-A.
Abstract from a doctoral dissertation, Ohio State University, 1965 (402p.).

D29. Hagood, Thomas Neal. "Elements of Humor in Ernest Hemingway." Dissertation Abstracts, Vol. 29 (March 1969), 3139-A.
Abstract from a doctoral dissertation, Louisiana State University, 1968 (275p.).

D30. Halliday, Ernest Milton. "Narrative Technique in the Novels of Ernest Hemingway." Microfilm Abstracts, Vol. 10 (1950), 110-111.
Abstract from a doctoral dissertation, University of Michigan, 1950 (316p.).

D31. Josephs, Mary Jim. "The Hunting Metaphor in Hemingway and Faulkner." Dissertation Abstracts International, Vol. 34 (September 1973), 1282-A.
Abstract from a doctoral dissertation, Michigan State University, 1973 (264p.).

D32. Kerr, Johnny F. "Hemingway's Use of Physical Setting and Stage Props in His Novels: A Study in Craftsmanship." Dissertation Abstracts, Vol. 26 (October 1965), 2217.
Abstract from a doctoral dissertation, Univer-

sity of Texas at Austin, 1965 (313p.).

D33.   Killinger, John Raymond, Jr.   "Hemingway and
the Dead Gods." American Doctoral Dissertations,
(1957), 121.
   Citation refers to a doctoral dissertation presented at the University of Kentucky, 1957.

D34.   Kobler, Jasper Fred, III.   "Journalist and Artist: The Dual Role of Ernest Hemingway." Dissertation Abstracts, Vol. 29 (August 1968), 606-
A to 607-A.
   Abstract from a doctoral dissertation, University of Texas at Austin, 1968 (228p.).

D35.   Kvam, Wayne Eugene.   "The Critical Reaction
to Hemingway in Germany, 1945-1965." Dissertation Abstracts International, Vol. 30 (September 1969), 1139-A to 1140-A.
   Abstract from a doctoral dissertation, University of Wisconsin, 1969 (410p.).

D36.   Laforest, Sister Mary Austina.   "Ernest Hemingway devant la critique française." American Doctoral Dissertations, (1963), 127.
   Citation refers to a doctoral dissertation presented at the Universite Laval (Canada), 1963.

D37.   Laurence, Frank Michael.   "The Film Adapta-
tions of Hemingway: Hollywood and the Hemingway Myth." Dissertation Abstracts International,
Vol. 31 (April 1971), 5411-A.
   Abstract from a doctoral dissertation, University of Pennsylvania, 1970 (418p.).

D38.   Lewis, Robert William, Jr.   "Eros and Agape:
Ernest Hemingway's Love Ethic." Dissertation
Abstracts, Vol. 24 (June 1964), 5411.
   Abstract from a doctoral dissertation, Univer-
sity of Illinois at Urbana-Champaign, 1963 (258p.).
This dissertation was published in a revised form
as Hemingway on Love See entry A29.

D39. Linderoth, Leon Walter. "The Female Characters of Ernest Hemingway." Dissertation Abstracts, Vol. 27 (October 1966), 1060-A.
Abstract of a doctoral dissertation, Florida
State University, 1966 (122p.).

D40. Lonie, Charles Anthony. "Accumulations of Silence: Survivor Psychology in Vonnegut, Twain
and Hemingway." Dissertation Abstracts International, Vol. 35 (June 1975), 7871-A.
Abstract of a doctoral dissertation, University
of Minnesota, 1974 (288p.).

D41. MacDonald, Scott M. "Narrative Perspective in
the Short Stories of Ernest Hemingway." American Doctoral Dissertations, (1970), 225.
Citation refers to a doctoral dissertation presented at the University of Florida, 1970.

D42. McLain, Charles Mansfield. "A Syntactic Study
of Four Non-Fiction Books by John Steinbeck and
Ernest Hemingway." Dissertation Abstracts International, Vol. 31 (March 1971), 4727-A.
Abstract from a doctoral dissertation, University of Colorado, 1970 (248p.).

D43. Matsuda, Sumio. "Symbolism and the Rhetoric
of Fiction in Hemingway's Novels." Dissertation
Abstracts, Vol. 28 (January 1968), 2689-A.
Abstract from a doctoral dissertation, University of Southern California, 1967 (274p.).

D44. Maynard, Reid Norris. "The Writer and Experience: Ernest Hemingway's Views on the Craft
of Fiction." Dissertation Abstracts International,
Vol. 31 (June 1971), 6620-A.
Abstract from a doctoral dissertation, University of California at Davis, 1970 (198p.).

D45. Mikhail, Mona Naguib. "Major Existentialist
Themes and Methods in the Short Fiction of
Idris, Mahfouz, Hemingway and Camus." Dis-
sertation Abstracts International, Vol. 33 (May

1975), 6320-A.
Abstract from a doctoral dissertation, University of Michigan, 1972 (192p.).

D46. Morrison, Robert William. "The Short Stories of Ernest Hemingway: A Search for Love and Identity." Dissertation Abstracts International, Vol. 30 (January 1970), 3018-A to 3019-A.
Abstract from a doctoral dissertation, Washington State University, 1969 (175p.).

D47. Nelson, Jon Eric. "Religious Experience in the Fiction of Ernest Hemingway." Dissertation Abstracts International, Vol. 31 (July 1970), 396-A.
Abstract from a doctoral dissertation, University of North Carolina at Chapel Hill, 1969 (236p.).

D48. Nucci, Joseph Charles. "The Poetry of Time and Place in the Fiction of Ernest Hemingway." Dissertation Abstracts International, Vol. 30 (August 1969), 733-A to 734-A.
Abstract from a doctoral dissertation, University of Pittsburgh, 1968 (261p.).

D49. O'Brien, Richard Michael. "Thematic Interrelation of the Concepts of Time and Thought in the Works of Ernest Hemingway." Dissertation Abstracts International, Vol. 31 (May 1971), 6066-A to 6067-A.
Abstract from a doctoral dissertation, New York University, 1969 (338p.).

D50. Oliver, Charles Montgomery, II. "Principles of 'True Felt Emotion' in Hemingway's Novels." Dissertation Abstracts International, Vol. 31 (March 1971), 4787-A.
Abstract from a doctoral dissertation, Bowling Green State University, 1970 (189p.).

D51. Pearson, Roger Luke. "The Play-Game Element in the Major Works of Ernest Hemingway." Dis-

sertation Abstracts International, Vol. 31 (June 1971), 6625-A to 6626-A.
Abstract from a doctoral dissertation, University of Massachusetts, 1970 (297p.).

D52. Pendleton, Harold Edmen. "Ernest Hemingway: A Theory of Learning." Dissertation Abstracts, Vol. 20 (February 1960), 3302-3303.
Abstract from a doctoral dissertation, University of Illinois, 1959 (330p.).

D53. Peterson, Richard Kenyon. "Hemingway: Direct and Oblique." Dissertation Abstracts, Vol. 22 (June 1962), 4353-4354.
Abstract from a doctoral dissertation, University of Washington, 1961 (316p.). Published in book form. See item C20.

D54. Raeburn, John Hay. "Ernest Hemingway: The Writer as Object of Public Attention." Dissertation Abstracts International, Vol. 30 (April 1970), 4462-A.
Abstract from a doctoral dissertation, University of Pennsylvania, 1969 (427p.).

D55. Reynolds, Michael Shane. "A Historical Study of Hemingway's A Farewell to Arms." Dissertation Abstracts International, Vol. 32 (September 1971), 1525-A to 1526-A.
Abstract from a doctoral dissertation, Duke University, 1971 (247p.).

D56. Robinson, Forrest Dean. "The Tragic Awareness of Hemingway's First Person Narrators: A Study of The Sun Also Rises and A Farewell to Arms." Dissertation Abstracts International, Vol. 27 (February 1967), 2543-A.
Abstract from a doctoral dissertation, Ohio University, 1966 (150p.).

D57. Rodnon, Stewart. "Sports, Sporting Codes and Sportsmanship in the Work of Ring Lardner, James T. Farrell, Ernest Hemingway and Wil-

liam Faulkner." Dissertation Abstracts, Vol. 23 (August 1962), 634-635.
Abstract from a doctoral dissertation, New York University, 1961 (197p.).

D58.   Rosen, Kenneth Mark. "Ernest Hemingway: The Function of Violence." Dissertation Abstracts International, Vol. 30 (June 1970), 5456-A.
Abstract from a doctoral dissertation, University of New Mexico, 1969 (219p.).

D59.   Ryan, Frank Leo. "Ernest Hemingway's Literary Reputation in America, 1924-1966." Dissertation Abstracts International, Vol. 36 (August 1975), 893-A.
Abstract from a doctoral dissertation, Catholic University of America, 1975 (278p.).

D60.   Shtogren, John Alexander, Jr. "Ernest Hemingway's Aesthetic Use of Journalism in His First Decade of Fiction." Dissertation Abstracts International, Vol. 32 (May 1972), 6454-A.

D61.   Simon, Charles. "The Literary Views and Attitudes of Ernest Hemingway." American Doctoral Dissertations, (1957), 119.
Citation refers to a doctoral dissertation presented at the University of Chicago, 1957.

D62.   Skenazy, Paul N. "Inarticulate Characters in Modern American Fiction: A Study of Fitzgerald, Hemingway and Faulkner." Dissertation Abstracts International, Vol. 34 (June 1974, 7783-A.
Abstract from a doctoral dissertation, Stanford University, 1974 (335p.).

D63.   Somers, Paul Preston, Jr. "Sherwood Anderson and Ernest Hemingway: Influences and Parallels." Dissertation Abstracts International, Vol. 32 (August 1971), 985-A.
Abstract from a doctoral dissertation, Pennsylvania State University, 1970 (198p.).

D64. Srivastava, Ramesh Kumar. "Hemingway's For Whom the Bell Tolls: A Critical Introduction with Annotations." Dissertation Abstracts International, Vol. 33 (January 1973), 3674-A. Abstract from a doctoral dissertation, University of Utah, 1972 (167p.).

D65. Stephens, Robert Oren. "The Escape Motif in the Works of Ernest Hemingway." Dissertation Abstracts, Vol. 19 (November 1958), 1079-1080. Abstract from a doctoral dissertation, University of Texas at Austin, 1958 (321p.).

D66. Stephenson, Edward Roger. "Stephen Crane and Ernest Hemingway: A Study in Literary Continuity." Dissertation Abstracts International, Vol. 33 (February 1973), 4433-A. Abstract from a doctoral dissertation, Brown University, 1972 (271p.).

D67. Sykes, Robert Howard. "Ernest Hemingway's Style: A Descriptive Analysis." Dissertation Abstracts, Vol. 24 (November 1963), 2043. Abstract from a doctoral dissertation, University of Pittsburgh, 1962 (316p.).

D68. Sylvester, Bickford. "Hemingway's Extended Vision: The Old Man and the Sea." Dissertation Abstracts, Vol. 27 (December 1966), 1841-A. Abstract from a doctoral dissertation, University of Washington, 1966 (196p.).

D69. Toop, Ronald Glenson. "Technique and Vision in the Fiction of Ernest Hemingway: A Chronological Study." Dissertation Abstracts International, Vol. 31 (February 1971), 4181-A to 4182-A. Abstract from a doctoral dissertation, University of Toronto, 1969.

D70. Vandiver, Samuel Earl. "The Architecture of Hemingway's Prose." Dissertation Abstracts, Vol. 28 (December 1967), 2268-A.

Abstract from a doctoral dissertation, University of Texas at Austin, 1967 (336p.).

D71. Walker, Emma Clement. "A Study of the Fiction of Hemingway and Faulkner in a College Sophomore English Class." Dissertation Abstracts International, Vol. 30 (April 1970), 4212-A.
Abstract from a doctoral dissertation, Ohio State University, 1969 (265p.).

D72. Wiese, Glen James. "Moral Vision in Hemingway's Fiction." Dissertation Abstracts International, Vol. 32 (April 1972), 5811-A.
Abstract from a doctoral dissertation, University of Utah, 1972 (173p.).

D73. Wylder, Delbert E. "Faces of the Hero: A Study of the Novels of Ernest Hemingway." Dissertation Abstracts International, Vol. 29 (May 1969), 4029-A to 4030-A.
Abstract from a doctoral dissertation, University of Iowa, 1968 (249p.). Also published in book form. See item C35.

D74. Wylder, Robert Clay. "An Investigation of Hemingway's Fictional Method, Its Sources and Its Influence on American Literature." Dissertation Abstracts, Vol. 15 (December 1955), 2535.
Abstract from a doctoral dissertation, University of Wisconsin, 1955 (368p.).

D75. Yokelson, Joseph Bernard. "Symbolism in the Fiction of Ernest Hemingway." Dissertation Abstracts, Vol. 23 (November 1962), 1714.
Abstract from a doctoral dissertation, Brown University, 1960 (196p.).

D76. Young, Leo Vernon. "Values of the Young Characters in the Fiction of Dos Passos, Hemingway, and Steinbeck." Dissertation Abstracts, Vol. 18 (February 1958), 518-519.
Abstract from a doctoral dissertation, Stanford University, 1957 (248p.).

D77. Young, Philip. "Ernest Hemingway and Huckle-
berry Finn: A Study in Continuity." American
Doctoral Dissertations, (1949), 149.
    Citation refers to a doctoral dissertation pre-
sented at the University of Iowa, 1949 (259p.).

(V, Dissertations and Theses, cont.)

MASTERS' THESES

Cited below are several master's theses that were culled from Masters Abstracts. Obviously this list reflects only a fraction of the theses that have been written about Ernest Hemingway.

D78.   Hagemann, Meyly Boratta. "Hemingway's Secret: Visual to Verbal Art." Masters Abstracts, Vol. 12 (September 1974), 267.
    Abstract from a master's thesis, University of Louisville, 1974 (99p.).

D79.   Korn, Gary Alan. "Hemingway's Women--Broken and Unbreakable." Masters Abstracts, Vol. 12 (December 1974), 431.
    Abstract from a master's thesis, Adelphi University, 1974 (57p.).

D80.   Kromi, Edythe Darlene. "Hemingway and the Aristotelian Tragedy." Masters Abstracts, Vol. 12 (December 1974), 431.
    Abstract from a master's thesis, North Texas State University, 1974 (133p.).

D81.   Lewis, Margaret Calien. "Ernest Hemingway's The Spanish War Dispatches from Spain, 1937-1938." Masters Abstracts, Vol. 3 (September 1970), 127.
    Abstract from a master's thesis, University of Louisville, 1969 (208p.).

D82.   Van Cader, Carol. "In a Sea of Hemingwaves:

A Study of the Relationship Between Hemingway's A Farewell to Arms and William Faulkner's Wild Palms." Masters Abstracts, Vol. 12 (September 1974), 269.

Abstract from a master's thesis, University of Louisville, 1973 (82p.).

VI

REVIEWS

Book reviews are mostly found in newspapers, periodicals or the more esoteric scholarly journals. They are helpful in giving one a critical perspective from those knowledgeable in the field of literature. The best way to find out what reviews have been written about a specific book is to consult one of the following indexes:

E1.   Book Review Digest. New York: H. W. Wilson, 1905- . Vol. 1- .

A current digest and index to reviews in English and American periodicals, arranged alphabetically by the author of the book reviewed, with title and subject indexes. Largely restricted to journals that review books as soon as they are published, rather than scholarly journals that publish reviews at a much later date.

E2.   Book Review Index. Detroit: Gale Research Co. , 1965- . Vol. 1- .

Covers a greater number and wider variety of periodicals than the Book Review Digest. Reviews are listed under author of the books reviewed.

E3.   Index to Book Reviews in the Humanities. Detroit: Phillip Thomson, 1960- . Vol. 1- .

Indexes reviews of books in English literature

(both creative work and critical studies), history, philosophy, and fine arts. Both scholarly and popular periodicals are included. Issued annually.

E4.   New York Times Book Review Index, 1896-1970.
      New York: Arno, 1973. V. 1+

Includes over 800,000 entries arranged as indexes by author, title, reviewer, subject and category.

In order to visualize the usefulness of these indexes some representative examples of reviews written on Hemingway's major works are listed below. The titles covered are arranged chronologically.

E5.   IN OUR TIME (1925).

Literary Review (October 17, 1927), 3.
New Republic, Vol. 45 (November 25, 1925), 22.
New York Times Book Review (October 18, 1925), 8.
New York World (October 18, 1925), 7m.
Springfield Republican (January 2, 1926), 7a.

E6.   THE TORRENTS OF SPRING (1926).

Books, New York Herald Tribune (July 18, 1926), 16.
Boston Transcript (July 3, 1926), 2.
Independent, Vol. 116 (June 12, 1926), 694.
International Book Review (October 1926), 667.
Literary Review (June 12, 1926), 9.
Nation, Vol. 123 (July 1928), 89.
New Republic, Vol. 48 (September 15, 1926), 101.
New York Times Book Review (June 13, 1926),

8.

New York World (May 30, 1926), 4m.
Outlook, Vol. 144 (September 15, 1926), 91.
Saturday Review of Literature, Vol. 3 (July
    31, 1926), 12.
Springfield Republican (August 29, 1926), 7f.

E7.   THE SUN ALSO RISES (1926).

Books, New York Herald Tribune (October 31,
    1926), 4.
Boston Transcript (November 6, 1926), 4.
Dial, Vol. 82 (January 1927), 73.
Independent, Vol. 117 (November 20, 1926),
    594.
Nation, Vol. 123 (December 15, 1926), 642.
New Republic, Vol. 49 (December 22, 1926),
    142.
New York Times Book Review (October 31,
    1926), 7; December 5, 1926), 5.
New York World (November 14, 1926), 10m.
Saturday Review of Literature, Vol. 3 (De-
    cember 11, 1926), 420; Vol. 3 (Decem-
    ber 18, 1926), 445.
Springfield Republican (November 18, 1926),
    7f.

E8.   MEN WITHOUT WOMEN (1927).

Booklist, Vol. 24 (January 1928), 163.
Bookman, Vol. 66 (September 1927), 87.
Books, New Herald Tribune (October 9, 1927),
    1.
Boston Transcript (January 7, 1928), 4.
Nation, Vol. 125 (November 16, 1927), 548.
New Statesman, Vol. 30 (November 26, 1927),
    208.
New York Evening Post (October 29, 1927),
    13.
New York Times Book Review (October 16,
    1927), 9.

North American Review, Vol. 224 (December
1927), adv.
Saturday Review of Literature, Vol. 4 (November 19, 1927), 322.
Springfield Republican (November 20, 1927),
7f.

E9. A FAREWELL TO ARMS (1929).

Booklist, Vol. 26 (December 1929), 119.
Books, New York Herald Tribune (October 6,
1929), 1.
Boston Transcript (October 19, 1929), 2.
Cleveland Open Shelf (November 1929), 143.
Nation, Vol. 129 (October 30, 1929), 497.
Nation and Athaneum, Vol. 46 (November 30,
1929), 319.
New Republic, Vol. 60 (October 9, 1929), 208.
New Statesman, Vol. 34 (November 30, 1929),
267.
New York Times Book Review (September 29,
1929), 5.
Outlook, Vol. 153 (October 16, 1929), 270.
Portland Evening News (October 15, 1929),
10.
Saturday Review, Vol. 148 (December 7, 1929),
684.
Saturday Review of Literature, Vol. 6 (Octo-
ber 12, 1929), 231.
Spectator, Vol. 143 (November 16, 1929), 727.
Springfield Republican (November 10, 1929),
7e.
Survey, Vol. 63 (November 1, 1929), 166.
Times [London] Literary Supplement, Novem-
ber 28, 1929), 998.
Yale Review, new series, Vol. 19 (winter
1930), vi.

E10.   DEATH IN THE AFTERNOON (1932).

Atlantic Bookshelf (November 1932), n. p.
Booklist, Vol. 29 (December 1932), 107.
Bookman, Vol. 75 (October 1932), 622.
Books (September 25, 1932), 3.
Boston Transcript (November 30, 1932), 3.
Forum, Vol. 88 (November 1932), ix.
Nation, Vol. 135 (November 9, 1932), 461.
New Republic, Vol. 73 (November 30, 1932),
    76.
New Statesman and Nation, Vol. 4 (December
    10, 1932), 738.
New York Times Book Review (September 25,
    1932), 5.
North American Review, Vol. 234 (December
    1932), 574.
Saturday Review of Literature, Vol. 9 (Septem-
    ber 24, 1932), 121.
Spectator, Vol. 149 (November 25, 1932), 761.
Springfield Republican (October 9, 1932), f3.
Times [London] Literary Supplement (December
    8, 1932), 936.
Yale Review, new series, Vol. 22 (winter
    1933), 390.

E11.   WINNER TAKE NOTHING (1933).

Books (October 29, 1933), 5.
Chicago Daily Tribune (October 28, 1933), 16.
Nation, Vol. 137 (November 15, 1933), 570.
New Republic, Vol. 77 (November 15, 1933),
    24.
New York Times Book Review (November 5,
    1933), 6.
North American Review, Vol. 237 (January
    1934), 94.
Saturday Review of Literature, Vol. 10 (Oc-
    tober 28, 1933), 217.
Springfield Republican (November 26, 1933),
    7e.

E12.   GREEN HILLS OF AFRICA (1935).

> Atlantic Bookshelf, Vol. 156 (November 1935),
>   30.
> Books (October 27, 1935), 3; (November 3,
>   1935), 18.
> Boston Transcript (October 30, 1935), 2.
> Chicago Daily Tribune (October 26, 1936), 15.
> Cleveland Open Shelf (October 1935), 17.
> Current History, Vol. 43 (December 1935),
>   xiv.
> Forum, Vol. 95 (January 1936), v.
> New Republic, Vol. 85 (November 27, 1935),
>   79; Vol. 85 (December 11, 1935), 135.
> New York Herald Tribune (October 25, 1935),
>   17.
> New York Times Book Review (October 27,
>   1935), 3.
> Saturday Review of Literature, Vol. 12 (Octo-
>   ber 26, 1935), 5.
> Springfield Republican (December 8, 1935), 7e.

E13.   TO HAVE AND TO HAVE NOT (1937).

> Atlantic (November 1937), n. p.
> Booklist, Vol. 34 (December 1, 1937), 129.
> Books (October 17, 1937), 3.
> Boston Transcript (October 30, 1937), 2.
> Canadian Forum, Vol. 17 (December, 1937),
>   322.
> Chicago Daily Tribune (October 16, 1937), 17.
> Forum, Vol. 98 (December 1937), 310.
> Manchester Guardian (October 15, 1937), 7.
> Nation, Vol. 145 (October 23, 1937), 439.
> New Republic, Vol. 92 (October 20, 1937),
>   305.
> New Statesman & Nation, Vol. 14 (October 16,
>   1937), 606.
> New York Times Book Review (October 17,
>   1937), 2.
> Saturday Review of Literature, Vol. 16 (Octo-
>   ber 16, 1937), 6; 8; Vol. 17 (November

6, 1937), 3.
Spectator, Vol. 159 (October 8, 1937), 7e.
Springfield Republican (October 17, 1937), 7e.
Time, Vol. 30 (October 18, 1937), 79.
Times [London] Literary Supplement (October
    9, 1937), 733.
Yale Review, new series, Vol. 27 (winter
    1938), vi.

E14. THE FIFTH COLUMN AND THE FIRST FORTY-
      NINE STORIES (1938).

Booklist, Vol. 35 (November 15, 1938), 98.
Books (October 16, 1938), 5.
Nation, Vol. 147 (December 10, 1938), 628.
New Republic, Vol. 96 (November 2, 1938),
    367.
New York Times Book Review (October 23,
    1938), 4.
New Yorker, Vol. 14 (October 22, 1938), 94.
Saturday Review of Literature, Vol. 18 (Oc-
    tober 15, 1938), 6.
Springfield Republican (November 6, 1938),
    7c.
Time, Vol. 32 (October 17, 1938), 75.

E15. FOR WHOM THE BELL TOLLS (1940).

Atlantic, n. v. (November 1940), n. p.
Booklist, Vol. 37 (November 1, 1940), 90.
Bookmark, Vol. 2 (January 1941), 12.
Books (October 20, 1940), 1.
Catholic World, Vol. 152 (January 1941), 502.
Commonweal, Vol. 33 (December 13, 1940),
    210.
Library Journal, Vol. 65 (November 1, 1940),
    923.
Nation, Vol. 151 (October 26, 1940), 395;
    (December 14, 1940), 609.
New Republic, Vol. 103 (October 28, 1940),
    591: Vol. 104 (January 20, 1941), 89.

New York Times Book Review (October 20, 1940), 1.
New Yorker, Vol. 16 (October 26, 1940), 82.
Saturday Review of Literature, Vol. 23 (October 26, 1940), 5.
Springfield Republican (October 27, 1940), 7e.
Time, Vol. 36 (October 21, 1940), 94.
Yale Review, new series, Vol. 30 (winter 1941), vi.

E16. ACROSS THE RIVER AND INTO THE TREES (1950).

Atlantic, Vol. 86 (October 1940), 80.
Booklist, Vol. 46 (July 15, 1940), 345; Vol. 47 (September 1, 1950), 13.
Bookmark, Vol. 10 (October 1950), 8.
Canadian Forum, Vol. 30 (November 1940), 190.
Catholic World, Vol. 172 (October 1950), 72.
Chicago Sun (September 10, 1950), 9.
Chicago Sunday Tribune (September 17, 1950), 3.
Christian Science Monitor (September 16, 1950), 11.
Commonweal, Vol. 52 (September 22, 1950), 585; Vol. 53 (November 3, 1950), 97.
Kirkus, Vol. 18 (July 15, 1950), 390.
Library Journal, Vol. 75 (September 1, 1950), 1407.
Manchester Guardian (September 8, 1950), 4.
Nation, Vol. 171 (September 9, 1950), 230.
New Republic, Vol. 123 (September 18, 1950), 20.
New Statesman & Nation, Vol. 40 (October 7, 1950), 343.
New York Herald Tribune Book Review (September 10, 1950), 1.
New York Times Book Review (September 10, 1950), 1.
New Yorker, Vol. 26 (September 9, 1950), 113.

San Francisco Chronicle (September 7, 1950),
18.

Saturday Review of Literature, Vol. 33 (September 9, 1950), 18; (October 28, 1950),
26.

Spectator, Vol. 184 (September 8, 1950), 279.

Springfield Republican (October 15, 1950), 19A.

Theatre Arts, Vol. 34 (November 1950), 5.

Time, Vol. 56 (September 11, 1950), 110.

Times [London] Literary Supplement (October
6, 1950), 628.

Yale Review, new series, Vol. 40 (autumn
1950), 191.

E17. THE OLD MAN AND THE SEA (1952).

Atlantic, Vol. 190 (September 1952), 72.

Booklist, Vol. 49 (September 1, 1952), 2.

Bookmark, Vol. 12 (October 1952), 10.

Canadian Forum, Vol. 32 (November 1952),
189.

Catholic World, Vol. 176 (November 1952),
151.

Chicago Sunday Tribune (September 7, 1952),
3.

Christian Science Monitor (September 11,
1952), 11.

Commonweal, Vol. 56 (September 19, 1952),
584.

Horn Book, Vol. 28 (December 1952), 427.

Kirkus, Vol. 20 (July 1, 1952), 377.

Library Journal, Vol. 77 (September 1, 1952),
1401.

Manchester Guardian (September 12, 1952), 4.

Nation, Vol. 175 (September 6, 1952), 194.

New Republic, Vol. 127 (October 6, 1952), 19.

New Statesman & Nation, Vol. 44 (September
13, 1952), 297.

New York Herald Tribune Book Review (September 7, 1952), 1.

New York Times Book Review (September 7,
1952), 1.

New Yorker, Vol. 28 (September 6, 1952),
115.
San Francisco Chronicle (September 7, 1952),
20.
Saturday Review, Vol. 35 (September 6, 1952),
10.
Spectator, Vol. 189 (September 12, 1952), 342.
Time, Vol. 60 (September 8, 1952), 114.
Times [London] Literary Supplement (September 12, 1952), 593.
Wisconsin Library Bulletin, Vol. 48 (September 1952), 215.
Yale Review, new series, Vol. 42 (autumn 1952), 8.

E18.   A MOVEABLE FEAST (1964).

America, Vol. 110 (May 16, 1964), 680.
American Literature, Vol. 36 (November 1964), 401.
Best Sellers, Vol. 24 (May 15, 1964), 69.
Book Week (May 3, 1964), 1.
Christian Century, Vol. 81 (May 6, 1964),
608.
Christian Science Monitor (May 14, 1964), 11.
Commonweal, Vol. 80 (May 29, 1964), 302.
Critic, Vol. 22 (June 1964), 58.
Encounter, Vol. 23 (July 1964), 71.
Harper, Vol. 228 (June 1964), 114.
Library Journal, Vol. 89 (April 1, 1964),
1610.
Nation, Vol. 198 (June 1, 1964), 560.
National Review, Vol. 16 (June 2, 1964), 450.
New Republic, Vol. 150 (May 9, 1964), 17.
New Statesman, Vol. 67 (May 22, 1964), 809.
New York Review of Books, Vol. 2 (June 11, 1964), 4.
New York Times Book Review (May 11, 1964),
1.
Newsweek, Vol. 63 (May 11, 1964), 102.
Reporter, Vol. 30 (June 4, 1964), 40.
Saturday Review, Vol. 47 (May 9, 1964), 29;

(December 5, 1964), 54.
Time, Vol. 83 (May 8, 1964), 98.
Times [London] Literary Supplement (May 21,
      1964), 425.

E19.   BY-LINE: ERNEST HEMINGWAY (1967).

Atlantic, Vol. 220 (July 1967), 109.
Best Sellers, Vol. 27 (July 1, 1967), 148.
Book Week (May 28, 1967), 6.
Christian Science Monitor (June 1, 1967), 15.
Commonweal, Vol. 86 (August 11, 1967), 499.
Critic, Vol. 26 (August 1967), 75.
Library Journal, Vol. 92 (May 1, 1967), 1834.
New Republic, Vol. 156 (June 10, 1967), 18.
New York Times Book Review (May 28, 1967),
      1.
New Yorker, Vol. 43 (June 3, 1967), 145.
Newsweek, Vol. 69 (June 5, 1967), 102.
Saturday Review, Vol. 50 (May 27, 1967), 23.
Time, Vol. 89 (May 19, 1967), 133.

E20.   ERNEST HEMINGWAY, CUB REPORTER (1970).

American Literature, Vol. 42 (November
      1970), 426.
Choice, Vol. 7 (November 1970), 1223.
Library Journal, Vol. 95 (April 1, 1970),
      1371.
Virginia Quarterly Review, Vol. 46 (autumn
      1970), cxxxvii.

E21.   ISLANDS IN THE STREAM (1970).

America, Vol. 123 (November 7, 1970), 382.
Atlantic, Vol. 226 (December 1970), 105.
Best Sellers, Vol. 30 (November 1, 1970),
      321.
Book World (October 11, 1970), 1.
Christian Science Monitor (October 8, 1970),

13.

Commentary, Vol. 50 (November 1970), 93.
Commonweal, Vol. 92 (October 23, 1970), 99.
Economist, Vol. 237 (October 10, 1970), 55.
Harper, Vol. 241 (October 1970), 120.
Library Journal, Vol. 95 (September 1, 1970),
    2827.
Nation, Vol. 211 (October 19, 1970), 376.
National Review, Vol. 22 (November 17, 1970),
    1214.
New Republic, Vol. 163 (October 10, 1970),
    25.
New Statesman, Vol. 80 (October 16, 1970),
    489.
New York Review of Books (October 8, 1970),
    17.
New York Times Book Review (October 4,
    1970), 1.
Newsweek, Vol. 76 (October 12, 1970), 118.
Saturday Review, Vol. 53 (October 10, 1970),
    23.
Time, Vol. 96 (October 5, 1970), 90.
Times [London] Literary Supplement (October
    16, 1970), 1193.

E22.   THE NICK ADAMS STORIES (1972).

Atlantic, Vol. 229 (June 1972), 98.
Best Sellers, Vol. 32 (May 1, 1972), 53.
Choice, Vol. 9 (September 1972), 814.
Library Journal, Vol. 97 (June 1, 1972),
    2116.
National Review, Vol. 24 (July 21, 1972),
    801.
Newsweek, Vol. 79 (April 17, 1972), 100B.
Virginia Quarterly Review, Vol. 48 (autumn
    1972), cxxi.

VII

AUDIO-VISUAL MATERIALS

Along with the books, articles and non-published source materials on Hemingway, the researcher will happily find a goodly number of audio-visual materials that will be helpful. Below is a brief list of sources useful in locating the titles for this chapter.

F1. Esner, A. G. S. Filmed Books and Plays: A List of Books and Plays from Which Films Have Been Made, 1928-1974, rev. ed. London: Andre Deutsch, 1972. 549p.
     Includes a film title index, an author index and a change of original title index.

F2. U. S. Library of Congress. Library of Congress Catalog-Motion Pictures and Filmstrips. Washington: U. S. Government Printing Office, 1953- . Vol. 1- .
     Includes entries for all motion pictures and filmstrips (but not for microfilm) currently cataloged or re-cataloged for the Library of Congress.

F3. U. S. Library of Congress. Library of Congress Catalog-Music and Phonorecords. Washington: U. S. Government Printing Office, 1953- . Vol. 1- .
     Contains entries for music scores, phonorecord including tape cassettes, etc.

NOVELS AND SHORT STORIES AS MOTION PICTURES

F4. A Farewell to Arms. Paramount Productions,

1932. Twentieth Century-Fox, 1957.

F5. Fiesta (The Sun Also Rises). Twentieth Century-Fox, 1957.

F6. For Whom the Bell Tolls. Paramount Productions, 1943.

F7. The Killers. Universal Motion Pictures, 1946; J. Arthur Rank Film Distributors, 1964.

F8. The Macomber Affair. Universal Motion Pictures, 1947.

F9. Under My Skin (My Old Man). Twentieth Century-Fox, 1950.

F10. The Old Man and the Sea. Warner Brothers Pictures, 1957.

F11. The Snows of Kilimanjaro. Twentieth Century-Fox, 1952.

F12. To Have and to Have Not. Warner Brothers, 1945 (reissued in 1950 under the title The Breaking Point); Seven Arts, 1958 (with the title The Gun Runners).

MOTION PICTURES ABOUT HEMINGWAY
OR ABOUT HIS BOOKS

F13. A Discussion of Ernest Hemingway's My Old Man. Encyclopaedia Britannica Educational Corp, 1970. Made by Larry Yust. 11 min. Sd. Color. 16mm (The Humanities short story showcase.) With teacher's guide. CREDITS: Collaborator, Clifton Fadiman. SUMMARY: Blake Nevius discusses the short story, My Old Man, by Ernest Hemingway. Uses footage from the original film to illustrate his points. (There was another issue in black and white.)

F14. Ernest Hemingway's Adventures of a Young Man.
Jerry Wald Productions. Released by Twentieth
Century-Fox Film Corp. , 1962. 145 min. Sd.
Color. 35mm. Cinema Scope. Color by De-
Luxe. CREDITS: Producer, Jerry Wald; direc-
tor, Martin Ritt; screenplay, A. E. Hotchner;
music, Franz Waxman; director of photography,
Lee Garmes; film editor, Hugh S. Fowler.
Cast: Richard Beymer, Diane Baker, Corinne
Calvet, Fred Clark, Dan Dailey, Paul Newman.
SUMMARY: An episodic drama which presents
a study of a young man who rebels against life
in a small Michigan village. Follows his adventures as a hobo, an advance agent for a burlesque
show, and a driver in an Italian ambulance ser-
vice during World War I, portraying the people
of various backgrounds who shaped his character.

F15. Hemingway. NBC. Released by McGraw-Hill
Book Co. , 1965. 54 min. Sd. B&W. 16mm.
With guide. SUMMARY: Demonstrates how the
life and work of Hemingway were independent,
revealing the deep roots of his art and outlook
and his participation in many of the important
events of the twentieth century.

F16. Hemingway's Spain--A Love Affair. American
Broadcasting Co. , 1968. 60 min. Sd. Color.
16mm. CREDITS: B. F. Goodrich Co. SUM-
MARY: A view of Spain as it was seen and de-
scribed by Ernest Hemingway in his books, The
Sun Also Rises, For Whom the Bell Tolls,
Death in the Afternoon, and The Dangerous Sum-
mer.

F17. Hemingway's Spain: Death in the Afternoon.
American Broadcasting Co. , Merchandising. Released by McGraw-Hill Book Co. , 1968. 15 min.
Sd. Color. 16mm. SUMMARY: Views of
people and places in Spain portrayed by Hemingway in his book by the same title. Follows the
widow of the author, Mrs. Mary Hemingway, as
she revisits the various locations.

F18.   Hemingway's Spain: For Whom the Bell Tolls.
        American Broadcasting Co. , Merchandising. Re-
        leased by McGraw-Hill Book Co. , 1968. 19 min.
        Sd. Color. 16mm. SUMMARY: Views of
        people and places in Spain portrayed by Heming-
        way in his novel of the same title. Follows the
        widow of the author, Mrs. Mary Hemingway, as
        she revisits the various locations.

F19.   Hemingway's Spain: The Sun Also Rises. A-
        merican Broadcasting Co. , Merchandising. Re-
        leased by McGraw-Hill Book Co. , 1968. 17 min.
        Sd. Color. 16mm. SUMMARY: Views of
        people and places in Spain portrayed by Heming-
        way in his novel of the same title. Follows the
        author's widow, Mrs. Mary Hemingway, as she
        revisits the various locations.

F20.   My Old Man, by Ernest Hemingway. Encyclo-
        paedia Britannica Educational Corp. , 1970.
        Made by Larry Yust. 27 min. Sd. Color.
        16mm. With teacher's guide. CREDITS: Col-
        laborator, Clifton Fadiman. SUMMARY: Pre-
        sents this short story by Hemingway using race
        track scenes and background footage filmed in
        Paris.

FILMSTRIPS

F21.   Ernest Hemingway. Schloat Productions, 1973.
        Made by Saga/Lumin/Foster Associates. 90 fr.
        color. 35 min. And phonodisc: 1 side, 331-3
        rpm. 14 min. (Great authors series.) With
        teacher's guide. CREDITS: Producer, Judith
        Buntz; writer, James Sage; consultant, S. C. V.
        Stetner; photographer, Rapho Guillumette. SUM-
        MARY: A study of the life and philosophy of
        Ernest Hemingway. Introduces some of his most
        important works.

F22.   Ernest Hemingway. Brunswick Productions Re-

leased by Educational Record Sales, 1971. 62
fr. Color. 35 min. (American novelists.)
SUMMARY: An illustrated biography of Hemingway with captions.

F23. Ernest Hemingway, the Man: A Biographical
Interpretation with Carlos Baker. Guidance Associates of Pleasantville, N.Y., 1968. 2 filmstrips (pt. 1, 82 fr; pt. 2, 84 fr.) Color. 35
min. And 2 phonodiscs: 12 in. 33 1/3 rpm.
Approx 16 min. each. Microgroove. With
teacher's manual. SUMMARY: Traces the life
of Ernest Hemingway, and relates events in his
life to specific portions of his work.

F24. Hemingway. Thomas S. Klise Co., 1970. 72
fr. Color. 35 min. And phonodisc: 2 sides
(1 side for manual projectors, 1 side for auto-
matic projectors), 12 in., 33 1/3 rpm. 18 min.
Microgroove. With script and bibliography.
CREDITS: Writer, marrater, and designer,
Thomas S. Klise. SUMMARY: A critical film
biography of Hemingway with special attention
to his earliest works, In Due Time and The Sun
Also Rises. Includes photographs from every
phase of Hemingway's life and work.

F25. Hemingway: His Life and Literature. Educational Dimensions Corp., 1975. 4 filmstrips (approx.
80 fr. each). Color. 35 min. And phonotape:
4 cassettes, approx. 18 min. each. With teacher's guide. SUMMARY: Covers Hemingway's
life and times and his specific works.

RECORDINGS

F26. Fiction in the Twenties: Fitzgerald and Hemingway. Santa Monica, Calif.: BFA Educational
Media, 197? F15006. 1 cassette. (American
literature series.) (Sussex tapes international.)
In container (19 x 19 x 2 cm). Booklet (7p.)

by A. Kazin and B. Lucid in container. CON-
TENTS: The Lost Generation: Ernest Heming-
way--The American Dream: F. Scott Fitzgerald.

F27. Grebstein, Sheldon Norman. For Whom the Bell
Tolls (Ernest Hemingway). Lecturer: Sheldon
N. Grebstein. Deland, Fla. : Everett/Edwards,
1970. 104. 1 cassette 2 1/2 x 4in. (20th Century American Novel.) (Cassette Curriculum.)
$12. 00. Title from container. Duration: 38
min.

F28. Hemingway, Ernest. Ernest Hemingway Reading.
Caedmon TC 1185. , 1965. 2 sides 12 in. 33
1/3 rpm. Microgroove. Recorded at Finca
Vigia, San Francisco de Paula, Cuba, 1948-1961.
Program notes by Mary Hemingway and A. E.
Hotchner on slipcase.

F28a. Hotchner, A. E. Hotchner on Hemingway. Sound
recording. Cincinnati, Writer's Voice, p1973.
no. 13. 1 cassette. Duration: 90 min. SUM-
MARY: A. E. Hotchner talks about his 14-year
friendship with Ernest Hemingway.

F29. Hynan, Patrick. Hemingway; A Sound Portrait.
Written and prepared by Patrick Hynan. Toronto, CBC Learning Systems, 1970. T56820-56823.
4 sides. 12 in. 33 1/3 rpm. Microgroove.
A condensation of recorded interviews with the
people who knew him best, or at least those who
were closest to him at various periods in his
life. Includes narrator, readings from his works,
and music background. Prepared for and originally broadcast on the radio network of the Canadian Broadcasting Corporation in 1970. An introduction to the recording by Malcolm Cowley
and program notes on album.

F30. Young, Philip. A Farewell to Arms (Ernest
Hemingway). Lecturer: Philip Young. Deland,
Fla. , Everett/Edwards, 1970. 110. 1 cassette.
2 1/2 x 4 in. (20th Century American Novel.)

(Cassette Curriculum.) $12. 00.   Title from con-
tainer.   Duration: 40 min.

F31. _____ . The Sun Also Rises (Ernest Hemingway).   Lecturer: Philip Young.   Deland, Fla. :
Everett /Edwards, 1971. 95. 1 cassette. 2 1/2
x 4 in.   (20th Century American Novel.) (Cassette Curriculum.) $12. 00.   Duration 30 min.

MUSIC

F32.   Jaroch, Jiri.   Starec a mare [The Old Man and
the Sea] Poema sinfonia dal romanzo di E. Hemingway.   Praha: Panton, 1964. vii p. , minia-
ture score (93p.).   (Kapesni partituns, sr. 59.)
Biographical and critical notes by Jiri Berkovec
in Czech, Russian, German, English, and French.
Duration: about 14 min.   (A Symphonic poem.)

VIII

REFERENCE AND MISCELLANEOUS SOURCES

Reference materials consist of those works that are designed to be consulted or referred to for some particular piece of information. These works are usually comprehensive in scope, condensed in treatment, and arranged in a special way to facilitate the ready and accurate location of information. Some of the more general reference materials that can be used for finding information on Ernest Hemingway have been discussed in previous chapters. This chapter will cover more specific reference materials and some related works.

BIBLIOGRAPHIES

G1.   Beebe, Maurice. "Criticism of Ernest Hemingway: A Selected Checklist with an Index to Studies of Separate Works," Modern Fiction Studies, Vol. 1 (August 1955), 36-45.

      An extensive listing up to the date of publication.

G2.   Bentz, Hans Willi. Ernest Hemingway in Übersetzungen. Ernest Hemingway Translated. Frankfurt a. M.: 1963. 34, 5p. (Weltliteratur in Übersetzungen. Reihe 8: Amerikanische Autoren, Bd. 1.)

      Lists translations of Hemingway's work in forty-five languages; includes translator, publisher, year published, and price. Also indexed by publisher, translator and language. Note: Numbered edition of 335 copies.

G3.   Bruccoli, Matthew Joseph. F. Scott Fitzgerald and Ernest Hemingway in Paris. With C. E. Frazer Clark, Jr. Catalogue of an exhibition at the Bibliothèque Benjamin Franklin in Paris, June 23-24, 1972, in conjunction with a conference at the Institut d'Etudes Américaines. 18p. 6x9 facsimilies.

Contains eighteen Hemingway items, including inscribed presentation copies, galley proofs, periodical containing first appearance, and letters. Only 650 copies of the exhibit catalogue were printed.

G4.   _____. Hemingway at Auction, 1930-1973. With C. E. Frazer Clark, Jr. Introduction by Charles W. Mann. Detroit: Gale Research Co., 1973. 286p.

This work reproduces pages from sixty auction sales and fifty-five dealers' catalogs containing books, letters, and manuscripts of Ernest Hemingway.

G5.   Cohn, Louis Henry. "Collecting Hemingway," Avocations, Vol. 1 (January 1938), 346-355.

The author comments on rare items and first editions of Hemingway's books. Includes photographs.

G6.   _____. A Bibliography of the Works of Ernest Hemingway. New York: Haskel House Publishers, 1973; Folcroft, Pa.: Folcroft Library Editions, 1973. 116p.

Both of these volumes are reprints of the 1931 edition published by Random House, New York. Up to the original date of publication this work was the most complete bibliography on Hemingway. The collations are very good including signatures and descriptions of dust wrappers.

G7.　Drew, Fraser B. "Thirty-five Years of Ernest Hemingway: A Catalogue of the Hemingway Collection of D. Fraser B. Drew" (mimeographed). Exhibited in the Edward H. Butler Library of the State University of New York College for Teachers at Buffalo, November 1-19, 1958. 8p.

Contains ninety-eight items, including inscribed first editions, periodicals containing first appearances, letters, photographs, and translations.

G8.　Ecsedy, Andorné. Ernest Hemingway Bibliográfia. With Eva Gáliczky. Budapest: Fövárosi Szabó Ervin Könyvtár, 1971. 54p.

A basic list of Hemingway's works in Hungarian. Includes illustrations.

G9.　Hanneman, Audre. Ernest Hemingway; A Comprehensive Bibliography. Princeton, N. J.: Princeton University Press, 1967. 568p. Supplement. Princeton, N. J.: Princeton University Press, 1975. 393p.

Both the main volume and the supplement are organized into three parts. The first is a descriptive and enumerative bibliography of Hemingway's work. The second is an enumerative biobibliography. The third part is the appendix and lists the place of publication of newspapers and periodicals cited within the body of the bibliography. Most of the sections are preceded by a brief introductory note covering usage, sources, and acknowledgments. Omissions to the first volume of the bibliography have been entered in each section of the supplement.

G10.　Koenig, Leigh W. "Ernest Hemingway: A Bibliographic Essay of Reference Sources" (mimeographed). River Forest, Ill.: Rosary College,

1971. 20 leaves.

A bibliographic essay discussing some 58 reference sources that contain information about Ernest Hemingway.

G11. Meriwether, James B. "The Text of Ernest Hemingway," Papers of the Bibliographical Society of America, Vol. 57 (October-December, 1963), 403-421.

The author discusses the need for a full-scale bibliographical and textual study of Hemingway's work.

G12. Monteiro, George. "Hemingway: Contribution Toward a Definitive Bibliography," Papers of the Bibliographical Society of America, Vol. 65 (October-December 1971), 411-414.

A checklist of work by and about Hemingway, translated into Portuguese.

G13. Mucharowski, Hans Günter. "Die Werke von Ernest Hemingway, eine Bibliographie der deutschsprachigen Hemingway-Literatur und der Originalwerke, von 1923 bis 1954" (mimeographed). Hamburg: 1955. 48 leaves

Covers his works published in the German language up to 1954.

G14. Oak Park Public Library. "Ernest Hemingway Collection." Oak Park, Ill.: Oak Park Public Library, 1974. 15p.

Includes about 140 titles some of which are annotated. Contains books, pamphlets, letters, and sundry items. Also lists biographical and critical materials, bibliographies and audio-visual materials.

G15. Orton, Vrest. "Some Notes Bibliographical and

Otherwise on the Books of Ernest Hemingway," Publishers Weekly, Vol. 117 (February 15, 1930), 884-886.

The author discusses Hemingway's major works up to this point and provides some valuable publication information along with a few insights.

G16. Pandolfi, Anna. "La Fortuna di Ernest Hemingway in Italia (1929-1961)," Studi Americani, Vol. 8 (1962), 151-199.

A bibliography of Italian translations and critical studies on pages 159-199.

G17. Richard Mary, Sister, O. P. "Addition to the Hemingway Bibliography," Papers of the Bibliographical Society of America, Vol. 59 (July-September, 1965), 327.

This brief article relates to Hemingway's letter on mutilated fish in Outdoor Life, Vol. 77 (June 1936). Author may be same as Sister Richard Mary Grimes [D28].

G18. Rogers, Jean Muir. "Bibliographical Notes on Hemingway's Men Without Women," Papers of the Bibliographical Society of America, Vol. 64 (April-June 1970), 210-213.

An analysis of the editions of Men Without Women for 1927, 1928, 1932, 1938, 1946, and 1955 for determination of weight differences and textual changes.

G19. Samuels, Lee. A Hemingway Checklist. New York: Scribner's, 1951. 63p.

A general listing of books, short stories, etc.

Includes a preface written by Hemingway.

G20. Stephens, Robert O. "Some Additions to the Hemingway Checklist," American Book Collector, Vol. 17 (April 1967), 9-10.

Lists materials not found in Samuel's bibliography and others.

G21. Triton College. Library. "A Compilation of Selected Doctoral Dissertation Abstracts, 1960-1972, on Ernest Hemingway, His Life and Works" (mimeographed). River Grove, Ill. : Triton College, [1974?]. 45 leaves (unnumbered).

Leaves 1-4 provide a listing of the dissertation abstracts included in the body of the bibliography. The remainder of this work includes the abstracts themselves. There appears to be no logical arrangement to the bibliography as all the abstracts are randomly presented.

G22. United States. Information Agency. "Ernest Hemingway: A Bibliography." Bonn: U.S. Information Agency, Office of the U.S. High Commissioner for Germany, 1954. 18p.

On page 5: a brief biography; pages 6-18 give a checklist of Hemingway's novels and short stories, with the latest German translations; anthologies containing his work; and biographical material along with criticism in books and periodicals.

G23. Wagner, Linda Welshimer. Ernest Hemingway: A Reference Guide. Boston: G. K. Hall, 1977. 383p.

This guide provides an annotated listing of secondary criticism of Hemingway's work. Approximately 2500 books, essays and reviews published from 1923 to 1975 are included. Many of the entries contain direct quotations from the work cited.

G24.   White, William. "Books about Hemingway A-
broad," American Book Collector, Vol. 18 (April
1968), 23.

A brief checklist of books written about Hemingway's foreign travels.

G25.   _____. "Ernest Hemingway and Nathanael
West: How Well-known Is Your Collector's
Item?," American Book Collector, Vol. 14 (May
1964), 29, 32.

A brief listing of Hemingway's more notable
collectables.

G26.   _____. "For Hemingway Buffs," American
Book Collector, Vol. 16 (May 1966), 27-28.

A list of recent books on and by Hemingway.

G27.   _____. "Hemingway in Korea," Papers of
the Bibliographical Society of America, Vol. 59
(April-June 1965), 190-192.

Lists a number of translations of Hemingway's
work.

G28.   _____. "Hemingway-iana: Annotated," Mark
Twain Journal, Vol. 11 (summer 1962), 11-12.

Provides notes on Hemingway's more promin-
ent works.

G29.   _____. The Merrill Checklist of Ernest Hemingway. Columbus, Ohio: Merrill, 1970. 45p.

A basic checklist of materials by Hemingway
and others about him.

G30.   _____. The Merrill Guide to Ernest Hemingway. Columbus, Ohio: Merrill, 1969. 44p.

A bio-bibliographical essay. Hemingway's Nobel Prize acceptance speech is reprinted on pages 28-29.

G31. _____. "Notes on Hemingway...," American Book Collector, Vol. 18 (January-February 1968), 30.

A brief listing of paperback reprints of books by and about Hemingway.

G32. _____. "On Collecting Hemingway," American Book Collector, Vol. 7 (November 1956), 21-23.

Discusses various items of interest in his Hemingway collection.

G33. _____. "Paperback Hemingway," American Book Collector, Vol. 15 (April 1965), 6.

A brief review of paperbacks of Hemingway's works and others about him.

G34. _____. "Why Collect Ernest Hemingway--or Anyone?," Prairie Schooner, Vol. 40 (fall 1966), 232-246.

White discusses his reasons for book collecting. He lists a number of Hemingway's works. Reprinted in American Book Collector, Vol. 18 (December 1966), 4-15.

G35. Young, Philip. The Hemingway Manuscripts; An Inventory. With Charles W. Mann. University Park, Pa.: Pennsylvania State University Press, 1969. 138p.

This volume lists some 332 items recovered from such places as a back room of Sloppy Joe's bar in Key West, from Cuba, and from Idaho. The 19,500 pages of manuscript, over 3,000 of which are unpublished, include drafts of a long sea novel; an autobiographical book about Africa; Garden of Eden, a novel set on the French Riviera; several Nick Adams short stories; and poems composed from 1939 through World War II. Inventory headings identify books, short fiction, journalism and other non-fiction, poetry, fragments, letters, miscellaneous, items, and copies of books and magazines.

G36.   Zink, D. D. "Ernest Hemingway. " Denver: U. S. Air Force Academy Library, 1959.   8p.   (Special bibliography series, no. 8.)

A very selective checklist of critical studies of Hemingway's writings.

MISCELLANEOUS SOURCES

G37.   Comprehensive Index to English-language Little Magazines, 1890-1970; Series One.   Edited by Marion Sader.   Milwood, N. Y. :   Kraus Thomson Organization, Ltd. , 1976.   8v.

An index to one hundred periodicals that are representative of the best of the various kinds of little magazines that flourished in the period 1890-1970.   The index is organized alphabetically according to the last name of the contributor or subject.   Each entry has been categorized as to type of work (i. e. , article, poem, illustration, etc.).   Full bibliographical information is provided for each entry.   Works by and about Ernest Hemingway are covered in volume 4, pages 1966-1970.

G38.   Fitzgerald-Hemingway Annual.   Washington: Microcard Editions, 1969- .   Vol. 1- .

This yearbook-type publication is devoted to writings by and about these two authors, with emphasis on the discovery of new material on or by both authors.

ERNEST HEMINGWAY: A CHRONOLOGY

1899:   Ernest Hemingway is born at Oak Park, Illinois, on 21 July.

1917:   Graduates from Oak Park High School.   Takes a job as reporter on the Kansas City Star.

1918:   Volunteers as ambulance driver with Red Cross.   Is assigned to Italian war theater. Receives severe wounds at Fossalta.

1919:   Returns home from the war.

1920:   Takes a job as feature writer for the Toronto Star Weekly.

1921:   Marries Hadley Richardson.   Goes to Paris with her.

1923:   Three Stories and Ten Poems is published in Paris.

1924:   In Our Time is published in Paris.

1925:   Begins a friendship with Scott Fitzgerald.   In Our Time is published by Boni and Liveright.

1926:   The Torrents of Spring and The Sun Also Rises are published by Charles Scribner's Sons.

1927:   Divorces Hadley and soon after marries Pauline Pfeiffer.   Men Without Women is published.

1928:   Makes his first visit to Key West, Florida. Hemingway's father commits suicide.

1929:   A Farewell to Arms is published.

1931:   Hemingway purchases house in Key West.

1932:   Death in the Afternoon is published.

1933:   Winner Take Nothing is published.

1933-34:   Hemingway and Pauline undertake a safari to East Africa.

1935:   Green Hills of Africa is published.

1936:   "The Short Happy Life of Francis Macomber" and "The Snows of Kilimanjaro" appear.

1937:   To Have and Have Not is published.

1937-38:   Covers the civil war in Spain as a newspaper correspondent.

1938:   The Fifth Column and the First Forty-nine Stories is published.

1940:   For Whom the Bell Tolls is published. Marries Martha Gellhorn several months after his divorce from Pauline. Purchases Finca Vigia, a house near Havana, Cuba.

1942:   Edits and writes introduction to Men at War.

1944:   As newspaper correspondent, covers Allied landing in Normandy, taking of Paris, and offensive into Germany.

1946:   Marries Mary Welch after his third marriage fails.

1950:   Across the River and Into the Trees is published.

1952:   The Old Man and the Sea is published.

1953:   Is awarded the Pulitzer Prize for Fiction.

1953-54: Takes a second hunting trip to East Africa. Is awarded the Nobel Prize for Literature.

1954:   Is badly hurt in two successive airplane accidents in Africa.

1959:   Purchases house at Ketchum, Idaho.

1961:   Hemingway commits suicide in house at Ketchum, on 2 July.

1964:   A Moveable Feast is published.

1972:   Islands in the Stream is published.

AUTHOR-TITLE INDEX

"Accumulations of Silence," C. A. Lonie D40

Across the River and into the Trees (Novel) B1; (Reviews) E16

Adams, Philip Duane, "Ernest Hemingway and the Painters" D1

"Addition to the Hemingway Bibliography," Sister Richard Mary G17

Alderman, Taylor. "Ernest Hemingway: Four Studies..." D2

Algren, Nelson. Notes from a Sea Diary A6

"American Anti-War Writers of World War I," J. J. Feeney D20

Anderson, Elizabeth. Miss Elizabeth A7

Apprenticeship of Ernest Hemingway, C. A. Fenton A17

"Architecture of Hemingway's Prose," S. E. Vandiver D70

Aristotelian Structure of a Farewell to Arms, J. J. Biles B3

"Armored Self," C. P. Gottlieb D24

Arnold, Lloyd R. High on the Wild with Hemingway

119

ingway: The Writer's Art of Self-Defense C9;
see also C14, C25

Bentz, Hans Willi. Ernest Hemingway in Übersetzungen G2

"Bibliographical Notes on Hemingway's Men Without Women," J. M. Rogers G18

Bibliography of the Works of Ernest Hemingway, L. H.
Cohn G6

Biles, J. I. The Aristotelian Structure of A Farewell
to Arms B3

Biography Index A2

Bishop, John P. "The Missing All," C39

Bobb, Sydney Ralph. "Fighter Against Loss: The Hemingway Hero," D5

Boehmer, Robert. See A39

Bonneville, Georges. Hemingway, "Pour qui sonne le
glas"; Analyse critique B9

Book Review Digest E1

Book Review Index E2

"Books about Hemingway Abroad," W. White G24

Bovie, Verne H. "The Evolution of a Myth," D6

Brady, Emily Kuempel. "The Literary Faulkner," D7

The Breaking Point (motion picture) F12

Broer, Lawrence Richard. "The Effects of Ernest
Hemingway's Identification with Certain Aspects
of Spanish Thinking..." (diss.) D8; Hemingway's
Spanish Tragedy A11

Brooks, Cleanth. The Hidden God C10

Browning, David Clayton. Everyman's Dictionary of
    Literary Biography A3

Bruccoli, Matthew Joseph. F. Scott Fitzgerald and
    Ernest Hemingway in Paris G3; Hemingway at
    Auction G4

By Force of Will, S. Donaldson C12

By-Line: Ernest Hemingway (non-fiction) B25; (re-
    views) E19

Byrd, Lemuel Brian. "Characterization in Ernest Hem-
    ingway's Fiction, 1925-1952," D9

Callaghan, Morley. That Summer in Paris A12

Carey, Gary. The Sun Also Rises; Notes B18

Carpenter, Frederick I. "Hemingway Achieves the
    Fifth Dimension," C40

Castillo Puche, José Luis. Hemingway in Spain A13

"Characterization in Ernest Hemingway's Fiction, 1925-
    1953," L. B. Byrd D9

Ciholas, Karin Nordenhaug. "Three Modern Parables,"
    D10

Cohen, Murray J. See B15

Cohn, Louis Henry. A Bibliography of the Works of
    Ernest Hemingway G6; "Collecting Hemingway,"
    G5

Collected Poems B42

"Collecting Hemingway," L. H. Cohn G5

Fussell, Edwin. "Hemingway and Mark Twain," C46

Galligan, Edward L. "Hemingway's Staying Power," C47

Gebhardt, Richard Coate. "Denial and Affirmation of Values in the Fiction of Ernest Hemingway," D21

Gellens, Jay. Twentieth Century Interpretation of A Farewell to Arms B5

Gladstein, Mimi Reisel. "The Indestructible Woman in the Works of Faulkner, Hemingway, and Steinbeck," D22

Gleaves, Edwin Sheffield, Jr. "The Spanish Influence on Ernest Hemingway's Concepts of Death, Nada, and Immortality," D23

Gottlieb, Carole Patricia. "The Armored Self," D24

Graham, John. "Ernest Hemingway" C48

Grant, Naomi M. "The Role of Women in the Fiction of Ernest Hemingway," D25

Grebstein, Sheldon Norman. For Whom the Bell Tolls (Ernest Hemingway) (recording) F27; Hemingway's Craft C13; The Merrill Studies in For Whom the Bell Tolls B11

Green Hills of Africa (non-fiction) B29; (reviews) E12

Greer, John Thomas. "The Limitations of the Concepts of Sin and Forgiveness as Reflected in the Writings of Ernest Hemingway," D26

Grimes, Larry E. "The 'Fifth Dimension': The Religious Design of Hemingway's Early Fiction," D27

Grimes, Sister Richard Mary [may be same as Richard

M. S. Reynolds D55

Hoffman, Frederick J. "No Beginning and No End: Hemingway and Death," C53

Hotchner, A. E. Hotchner on Hemingway (cassette) F28a; Papa Hemingway: A Personal Memoir A23

Hovey, Richard Bennett. Hemingway: The Inward Terrain A24

How It Was, M. W. Hemingway A21

Howell, John M. Hemingway's African Stories B35, C15

"Hunting Metaphor in Hemingway and Faulkner," M. J. Josephs D31

Hynan, Patrick. Hemingway: A Sound Portrait (recording) F29

"Immortal Hemingway: Letter and Other Manuscript Material," W. Rodger C59

In Our Time (reviews) E5; (short stories) B36

"In a Sea of Hemingwaves," C. Van Cader D82

"Inarticulate Characters in Modern American Fiction," P. N. Skenazy D62

"Indestructible Women in the Works of Faulkner, Hemingway, and Steinbeck," M. R. Gladstein D22

Index to Book Reviews in the Humanities E3

"Investigation of Hemingway's Fictional Method," R. C. Wylder D74

"Ironic Vision in Hemingway's Short Stories," C. W.

"Lost Ladies," S. W. Dean D14

McCaffery, John K. M., ed. Ernest Hemingway A30, C18

MacDonald, Scott M. "Narrative Perspective in the Short Stories of Ernest Hemingway," D41

Machlin, Milton. The Private Hell of Hemingway A31

McLain, Charles Mansfield. "A Syntactic Study of Four Non-Fiction Books by John Steinbeck and Ernest Hemingway," D42

McLendon, James. Papa: Hemingway in Key West A32

The Macomber Affair (motion picture) F8

Magill, Frank N. Cyclopedia of World Authors A5

Mailer, Norman. See A19

"Major Existentialist Themes and Methods in the Short Fiction of Idris, Mahfouz, Hemingway and Camus," M. N. Mikhail D45

Major Works of Ernest Hemingway, S. Cooperman B19

Mann, Charles W. See G35

"Mark of Sherwood Anderson on Hemingway," P. P. Somers C62

Matsuda, Sumio. "Symbolism and the Rhetoric of Fiction in Hemingway's Novels," D43

Maynard, Reid Norris. "The Writer and Experience," D44

Men at War (edited work) B48

Men Without Women (reviews) E8; (short stories) B37

Meriwether, James B. "The Text of Ernest Hemingway,"
G11

Merrill Checklist of Ernest Hemingway, W. White G29

Merrill Guide to Ernest Hemingway, W. White G30

Merrill Studies in For Whom the Bell Tolls, S. N. Grebstein B11

Mikhail, Mona Naguib. "Major Existentialist Themes and
Methods in the Short Fiction of Idris, Mahfouz,
Hemingway and Camus," D45

Miller, Madelaine Hemingway. Ernest Hemingway's Sister, "Sunny," Remembers A33

Miss Elizabeth; A Memoir, E. Anderson A7

"The Missing All," J. P. Bishop C39

Mizener, Arthur. Twelve Great American Novels B22

Modern American Literature, D. N. Curley C3

Monteiro, George. "Hemingway: Contribution Toward a
Definitive Bibliography," G12

Montgomery, Constance Cappel. Hemingway in Michigan
A34

Moore, Harry T. See C13

"Moral Vision in Hemingway's Fiction," G. J. Wiese D72

Morrison, Robert William. "The Short Stories of Ernest
Hemingway," D46

A Moveable Feast (non-fiction) B30; (reviews) E18

Mucharowski, Hans Günter. Die Werke von Ernest Hemingway G13

My Brother Ernest Hemingway, L. Hemingway A20

My Friend, Ernest Hemingway, W. W. Seward A44

My Old Man by Ernest Hemingway (motion picture) F20

Nahal, Chaman Lal. The Narrative Pattern in Ernest
Hemingway's Fiction C19

The Narrative Pattern in Ernest Hemingway's Fiction, C.
L. Nahal C19

"Narrative Perspective in the Short Stories of Ernest Hemingway," D41

"Narrative Technique in the Novels of Ernest Hemingway,"
E. M. Halliday D30

Nelson, Jon Eric. "Religious Experience in the Fiction of
Ernest Hemingway," D47

New York Times Book Review Index, 1896-1970 E4

The Nick Adams Stories (reviews) E22; (short stories)
B38

"No Beginning and No End: Hemingway and Death," F. J.
Hoffman C53

Nolan, William F. Hemingway, Last Days of the Lion
A35

Notes from a Sea Diary, N. Algren A6

"Notes on Hemingway," W. White G31

Nucci, Joseph Charles. "The Poetry of Time and Place in
the Fiction of Ernest Hemingway," D48

Oak Park Public Library. Ernest Hemingway Collection
G14

Simon, Charles. "The Literary Views and Attitudes of Ernest Hemingway," D61

Singer, Kurt D. Ernest Hemingway, Man of Courage A46; Hemingway: Life and Death of a Giant A47

Skenazy, Paul N. "Inarticulate Characters in Modern American Fiction," D62

The Snows of Kilimanjaro (motion picture) F11

The Snows of Kilimanjaro and Other Stories, C. Hille-gass B34

Sokoloff, Alice Hunt. Hadley, the First Mrs. Heming-way A48

"Some Additions to the Hemingway Checklist," R. O. Stephens G20

"Some Notes Bibliographical and Otherwise on the Books of Ernest Hemingway," V. Orton G15

Somers, Paul Preston, Jr. "Mark of Sherwood Anderson on Hemingway," C62; "Sherwood Anderson and Ernest Hemingway" (diss.) D63

The Spanish Earth (film script) B47

"Spanish Influence on Ernest Hemingway's Concepts of Death, Nada, and Immortality," E. S. Gleaves D23

"Sports, Sporting Codes and Sportsmanship in the Work of Ring Lardner, James T. Farrell, Ernest Hemingway and William Faulkner," S. Rodnon D57

Srivastava, Ramesh Kumar. Determinism in Hemingway C26; "Hemingway's For Whom the Bell Tolls," (diss.) D64

Starec a Mare, J. Jaroch (music) F32

"Stephen Crane and Ernest Hemingway," E. R. Stephenson D66

Stephens, Robert Oren. "The Escape Motif in the Works of Ernest Hemingway" (diss.) D65; Hemingway's Nonfiction C27; "Some Additions to the Hemingway Checklist," G20

Stephenson, Edward Roger. "Stephen Crane and Ernest Hemingway," D66

Straumann, Heinrich. See C4

"A Study of Hemingway's For Whom the Bell Tolls," R. D. Crozier D11

"Study of the Fiction of Hemingway and Faulkner," E. C. Walker D71

The Sun Also Rises (novel) B17; (reviews) E7

The Sun Also Rises (Ernest Hemingway), P. Young (cassette) F31

The Sun Also Rises: Notes, G. Carey B18

The Sun Also Rises; Notes, C. K. Hillegass B20

Sykes, Robert Howard. "Ernest Hemingway's Style," D67

Sylvester, Bickford. "Hemingway's Extended Vision," D68

"Symbolism and the Rhetoric of Fiction in Hemingway's Novels," S. Matsuda D43

"Symbolism in the Fiction of Ernest Hemingway," J. B. Yokelson D75

"Syntactic Study of Four Non-Fiction Books by John Steinbeck and Ernest Hemingway," C. M. McLain D42

"Technique and Vision in the Fiction of Ernest Hemingway," R. G. Toop D69

"Text of Ernest Hemingway," J. B. Meriwether G11

That Summer in Paris, M. Callaghan A12

"Thematic Interrelation of the Concepts of Time and Thought in the Works of Ernest Hemingway," R. M. O'Brien D49

"Theme of Individualization in the Short Stories of Ernest Hemingway," J. M. DeFalco D15

Thirty-five Years of Ernest Hemingway, F. B. Drew G7

"Three Modern Parables," K. N. Ciholas D10

Three Stories ... and Ten Poems B43

Three Stories: Up in Michigan, Out of Season, My Old Man and Ten Poems B40

To Have and to Have Not (motion picture) F12; (novel) B23; (reviews) E13

Today Is Friday (play) B46

Toop, Ronald Glenson. "Technique and Vision in the Fiction of Ernest Hemingway," D69

The Torrents of Spring (novel) B24; (reviews) E6

"Tragic Awareness of Hemingway's First Person Narrators," F. D. Robinson D56

Traver, Robert. See A33

Triton College. Library. A Compilation of Selected Doctoral Dissertation Abstracts, 1960-1972, on Ernest Hemingway G21